FEDERICO GARCÍA LORCA:
IMPOSSIBLE THEATER

FEDERICO GARCÍA LORCA:
IMPOSSIBLE THEATER

Five plays and thirteen poems
by Federico García Lorca

In new translations by Caridad Svich

GREAT TRANSLATIONS SERIES

A Smith and Kraus Book

Published by
Smith and Kraus, Inc.
177 Lyme Road, Hanover, NH 03755
www.SmithKraus.com

Cover and Text Design by Julia Hill Gignoux, Freedom Hill Design
Cover Art by Frederic Amat, from his film *Trip to the Moon.*

First edition: August 2000
10 9 8 7 6 5 4 3 2 1

Library of Congress Cataloging-in-Publication Data

García Lorca, Federico, 1898–1936.
[Selections. English. 2000]
Federico García Lorca : impossible theater : five plays and thirteen poems / by
Federico García Lorca ; in new translations by Caridad Svich. —1st ed.
p. cm. — (Great translations series)
Includes bibliographical references.
ISBN 1-57525-228-7
I. Svich, Caridad. II. Title. III. Great translations for actors series.

PQ6613.A763 A6 2000
868'.6209—dc21   00-044571

CONTENTS

Special thanks to
Shelley Berc, Michael Dixon, Sebastian Doggart,
Jessica Dufresne, Ted Gerney,
Esther Lopez and everyone at Television-Ovideo,
Mark Taper Forum Theater, Linda Nicol,
University of California-San Diego Department of Theater,
and Craig Watson.

As always, this is for my parents.

FEDERICO GARCÍA LORCA:
AN ICON FOR EVERY AGE

By Maria Delgado
Queen Mary & Westfield College, University of London

El teatro fué siempre mi vocación. He dado al teatro muchas horas de mi vida. Tengo un concepto del teatro, en cierta forma personal y resistente. El teatro es la poesia que se levanta del libro y se hace humana. Y al hacerse habla y grita, llora y desespera. El teatro necesita que los personajes que aparezcan en la escena lleven un traje de poesía y al mismo tiempo que se les vea los huesos, la sangre.... Hoy en España la generalidad de los autores y de los actores ocupan una zona apenas intermedia. Se escribe en el teatro para el piso principal y se quedan sin satisfacer la parte de butacas y los pisos del paraíso. Escribir para el piso principal es lo más triste del mundo... Yo en el teatro he seguido una trayectoria definida. Mis primeras comedias son irrepresentables.... En estas comedias imposibles está mi verdadero propósito. Pero para demonstrar una personalidad y y tener derecho al respeto, he dado otras cosas. (Federico García Lorca, 1936)[1]

(The theater was always my vocation. I've given the theater many hours of my life. I have a concept of theater, which is, in a certain way, personal and strong. The theater is poetry which rises up from the page and is made human. And when this happens it talks and shouts, cries and despairs. The theater requires that the characters who appear on stage be dressed as poetry and at the same time we should see their bones, their blood....Today in Spain the majority of writers and actors occupy a barely intervening role. Theater is written for the dress circle and the stalls and balcony remain unsatisfied. Writing for the dress circle is the saddest thing in the world... I've tried to follow a clearly defined theatrical journey. My first plays were unrepresentable.... In these impossible plays lie my real intentions. But to demonstrate a personality and gain the right to respect, I've written other things.)

In his autobiography, *My Last Breath*, the Spanish filmmaker Luis Buñuel refers to Federico García Lorca as "brilliant and charming, the finest of all human beings I've ever known. He was his own masterpiece."[2] An early martyr of the Franco regime—shot by nationalist troops soon after the military uprising in July 1936 that was to plunge Spain into civil war for three years, García Lorca's name has consequently stood as a potent symbol of a liberal era brutally brought down by an illegitimate alliance of repressive elements keen to curb the path of change on which the elected left-wing Popular Front government was decisively embarking. He now stands as a popular and academic icon of twentieth-century Spanish culture, whose works enjoy a malleability that allows them to be processed, appropriated, and reinterpreted by the demands of each age. García Lorca has now entered the realm of the classics: a continuing site of struggle, where conflicts are played out at particular social and cultural moments in specific geographical locations. His resonance is visible not only in the visceral rhythms of dramatist Sam Shepard, the haunting elegies of Pablo Neruda, and the narrative of Pedro Almodóvar's ninth film *High Heels* (1991; based, according to the filmmaker, on *The House of Bernarda Alba*), but also on all who have gone on to forge an artistic practice that is profoundly engaged with the social and theatrical dilemmas of the time without ever appearing didactic or sentimental.

Although primarily recognized as a playwright and a poet, García Lorca was also an accomplished pianist, painter, and stage director whose collaborations with performers Margarita Xirgu, Josefina de Artigas, and the state-funded touring theater company La Barraca were to introduce innovative models of stage practice that moved resolutely away from the constraints of naturalism toward what García Lorca himself termed "el nuevo teatro, avanzando de formas y teoría"[3] (the new theater, advancing forms, and theory). As both playwright and director, he consistently challenged the parameters of what was possible on a stage, providing an avant-garde aesthetic where texture, shape, and shifts of tone are accorded equal importance to thematic considerations. In crafting a lyrical dramatic language that is musical in its precision and economy, García Lorca moved toward a model of theater that dispenses with the literal in favor of imaginative excess.

Once wryly referred to by the Argentine writer Jorge Luis Borges as "a professional Andalusian,"[4] there has been a critical tendency to celebrate the work rooted in the southern landscape of his birth that has been read rather too exclusively through accessible folkloric cliches and populist myths of the region as a land of fiery flamenco and guitar-strumming, castanet-clicking gypsies. It is especially the association of García Lorca's most celebrated dramatic work—the rural trilogy of *Bodas de sangre* / *Blood Wedding, Yerma*, and *La casa de Bernarda Alba* / *The House of Bernarda Alba*—with the Andalusian landscape and culture that has provided a recognizable point of contact for a foreign readership. The fact that Spain's cultural construction has been irrevocably linked with the culture of flamenco for about two hundred years has allowed García Lorca's Andalusian-located work to be read and marketed through potent stereotypes that may not be applied with the same ease to the work of contemporaries like Ramón del Valle-Inclan or successors like Francisco Nieva. Certainly the historical, cultural, and physical landscapes of Andalusia were to have a profound influence on his writing. García Lorca's dramatic world is undeniably rooted in a rural environment where characters constantly make reference to rural iconography to present their own sense of angst and desperation. Nevertheless whilst it shaped his pictorial and literary imagination, García Lorca's work cannot ever be simply reduced to that arid rural milieu. Although infused by his native Granada, the richness of his writing comes as much from the traditions of earlier generations of poets like Luis de Góngora and Garcilaso de la Vega, his period at Madrid's Oxbridge-like Residencia de Estudiantes in the 1920s with the two *enfant terribles* of twentieth-century surrealism Luis Buñuel and Salvador Dalí, his travels to New York and Cuba between 1929 and 1930, and the pioneering work of his contemporaries like Ramón del Valle-Inclán and Manuel de Falla.

As one of the first martyrs of the Civil War, García Lorca creates a romantic subject for exploitation—appropriated by the left and denigrated by the right, he has functioned as a symbol of all that was lost with the defeat of the Republican forces in 1939. Generating conspicuous critical attention, he has inspired two rigorous English-language biographies.[5] From the studied brooding pose of Gibson's formal cover photograph to the playful flamboyant portrait of Leslie Stanton's more recent publication, he gazes out at the reader, both subject and object, made into a fetish and preserved in an eternally youthful image of attractive, elusive allure.

During the 1980s and 1990s more oblique works like *El público* / *The Public,* and *Así que pasen cinco años* / *As Five Years Pass* and the shorter plays collected in this volume have come to question the "Andalusian" García Lorca whose rural trilogy and *Romancero gitano* / *Gypsy Ballads* have been read as a mirror of his much publicized life, as reflections of Andalusian life during the 1920s and 1930s, as elegies where his own death is anticipated, and as metaphors for his homosexuality, demonstrating how sexual and social deviancy lead to destruction.

With Spanish director Lluís Pasqual's seminal productions of *El público*

/ *The Audience* in 1986 and *Comedia sin título* / *Play without a Title* in 1989 as well as Miguel Narros' staging of *Así que pasen cinco años* / *As Five Years Pass* also in 1989, focus shifted to dramatic works that had been hitherto regarded as peripheral or "impossible." Both a process of reappropriation and scholarship, the staging of these unfamiliar works served to re-envisage García Lorca, introducing audiences to a largely unknown section of his repertoire. The plays included in this volume, like *El paseo de Buster Keaton* / *Buster Keaton Takes a Walk*, and *La doncella, el marinero y el estudiante* / *The Maiden, the Sailor, and the Student* form part of this "unknown" García Lorca. Occupying an uneasy space between film and performance script, they challenge the reassuring tendencies of the realist play. Rather, their playful interrogations of linguistic certainty and dramatic norms serve to position García Lorca as a theatrical innovator within the European avant-garde of the 1920s who were to consciously flaunt the rules that had hitherto governed dramatic construction. Like Bertolt Brecht, García Lorca's work as a director brought him into contact with some of the theatrical practitioners who were moving away from the rather outdated nineteenth-century models of theatrical composition toward a more musical form of dramaturgy: A stage practice tied to European modernism and its rupturing of linear narrative structures. Here the human figure merges with the stage landscape to take over new explorations of dramatic space. These dramatic experiments, referred to by García Lorca in the epigraph I cite, clearly demonstrated an alternative direction toward metatheater that interrogates the very foundations of the discipline.

In their celebration of the ephemerality of performance, the plays collected here signal an acknowledgement of the breathing, kinetic relationship between the moving living body and its performance environment. The exploration of spectatorship in both *Don Perlimplín* and *Así que pasen cinco años* / *As Five Years Pass* and García Lorca's screenplay, *Viaje a la luna* / *A Trip to the Moon*, situates these works within an evolving fascination with ways of seeing, an investigation of the gaze, and new vocabularies and questions of perception probed by surrealism and other modernist movements in the aftermath of the first World War. Techniques developed and motifs located within these works were to be picked up on in the site-specific and environmental theater of the 1960s that probed and rethought the boundaries around theater, dance, and the visual arts, reconfiguring dramatic focus around the place of performance while asking decisive questions around the exposure and politics of the gaze. Often we, as readers, are made aware of a wide spectrum of spectating positions. Our gaze is diverted, disturbed, shifted and probed. The masquerading bodies conjured by García Lorca, serve as metaphors for a range of elusive desires and compromised allegiances. Gender and sexuality become the site of role play, never taken as a given but rather elegantly displayed as constructed artifice. Bodies are deconstructed and reconfigured. Perhaps, as in the work of Tony Kushner, overt theatricality becomes the prism through which both characters and audience are given a threshold of revelation.[6] Within the stage's defined space, identities are mapped. The navigation of social and cultural boundaries becomes the terrain around which each of these works is set.

For painters and scenographers alike, García Lorca's work has provided the canvas on which to create diverse landscapes of memory, experience, and displacement. Drawing on past traditions configured within a cultural present, Salvador Dalí, Fabià Puigserver, and Frederic Amat have all reshaped scenographic vocabulary through metaphoric sets that have built on bodies of inherited cultures to provide radical configurations of shape, texture, and perspective. García Lorca's textual landscapes have been the site for some of the most exciting theatrical experiments of recent times. Peter Brook has referred to the canvas membrame set that Fabià Puigserver created for Victor García's 1970 production of *Yerma* as one of the definitive moments of twentieth-century stage design.[7] The flexibility of García Lorca's stage directions allows for imaginative location and the last twenty years has seen productions of these works (a significant percentage of which were unpublished at the time of García Lorca's death[8]) move away from mimetic realism and representational theater toward visually striking productions that have sought to highlight the structures of signification at play in the works whilst situating the performer as part of an ever-shifting visual and aural landscape. The pairing of Nuyorican director Michael John Garcés with this new translation of *As Five Years Pass* for INTAR's "100 Years of Lorca" season in 1998 served to "intrigue" *Village Voice* critic Ed Morales precisely because rather than present García Lorca as a dramatist imprisoned in the mythology of a rural Andalusia, "obscuring his contemporary relevance,"[9] the production attempted to point to the play's status as a site of continuing ideological struggles. Negating a simplistic reading that equates the Young Man with García Lorca, the production sought to tease out the tensions and contradictions present when a work of the European avant-garde is presented in a cultural, linguistic, social, and political climate distinct from that which engendered it.

When García Lorca first read *Así que pasen cinco años / As Five Years Pass* to actress Margarita Xirgu in Madrid's El Pardo in 1930, she viewed it as unstageable. Years later she was to state her desire to see it staged with set designs by Salvador Dalí.[10] This was never to happen but the imaginary pairing of García Lorca's ambitious play with surrealism's most flamboyant exponent by one of the most influential performers of the first half of the twentieth century indicates the need for stage practice to reimagine perceptions of time and space as well as the relationship between representation and the real. That this enigmatic play was only first performed in Spain in 1978, forty-seven years after it was written, displays the problematic dialogue between these difficult works and theatrical conventions that have languished behind experiments in the other visual arts. Rather than tell stories, these plays prioritize the theatrical experience itself with its inherent reliance on audience reciprocity and reflection. Following on these experiments in conceptual art, García Lorca recognized the diverse subjectivities that we bring to the texts we read. In *Viaje a la luna / A Trip to the Moon* and *Así que pasen cinco años/As Five Years Pass* especially, the pictorial space of performance evolves before our eyes in a brutal interrogation of the reality of reality. In Amat's sumptuous 1998 film of *Viaje a la luna/A Trip to the Moon,* García Lorca's only screenplay written in New York between 1929 and 1930 as a rebuff to his friend Buñuel's 1928 film *Un chien andalou,* new technologies blur the interaction of live bodies and animation. The screenplay's vocabulary is clearly grounded in the avant-garde that engendered Buñuel and Dalí's work, but in the hands of first-time director Amat, it is a sumptuous journey in filmmaking: a testament to past and present traditions, a visual poem of breathtaking beauty where desire and its discontents determines both content and form. An array of images flicker across the screen; patterns of light, texture, and color are juxtaposed with a score by composer Pascal Comelade where the interplay of tones and rhythms leave their indelible mark on the screen as the viewer's imagination negotiates that what Bonnie Marranca, paraphrasing Herbert Blau calls, "that transcendent moment in which theater, or any other practice, changes, as ideology itself does, into something other that what it appeared to be."[11]

The works collected in this volume encapsulate the very tensions and excesses of our existence: the private and the public, the personal and the political, masculinity and femininity, location and dislocation, those shifting parameters through which our daily life is constantly redefined. Lorca's characterizations move away from stereotypes and demonstrate the way in which the roles we play are all shaped and conditioned by the ideologies of the societies we inhabit. For those who would see *La casa de Bernarda Alba / The House of Bernarda Alba*, his final and perhaps most resonant play, as a study of dictatorial oppression and intimidation, the views of stage director Pedro Alvarez Osorio that the first initials of the daughters' names spell out a dedication 'a mama'—to mother—suggests the ambiguity both of a persona and a play that consistently resists easy categorization.[12] For a writer whose correspondence, plays, and poems revolve around the presentation of a series of complex co-existing identities, is it perhaps not surprising that his final testament to his beloved mother should be a dark, claustrophobic, and elusive domestic drama in whose interplay of silence and malicious accusations lie a bitter microcosm of the larger conflicts played out on the country's political stages that were to erupt in a fratricidal civil war, scars of which still haunt the national psyche.

[1] Federico García Lorca, from an interview with Felipe Morales, 1936, in *Obras completas*, ed Arturo del Hoyo (Madrid: Aguilar, 1957), pp. 1634–1635.

[2] Luis Buñuel, *My Last Breath*, trans. Abigail Israel (London: Flamingo/Fontana Paperbacks, 1985), p. 158.

[3] Federico García Lorca, from an interview in New York, 1931, in *Obras completas*, p. 1608.

[4] John London, *The Unknown Federico García Lorca* (London: Atlas Press, 1996), p. 7.

[5] Ian Gibson, *Federico García Lorca: A Life* (New York: Pantheon Books, 1989) and Leslie Stainton, *Lorca: A Dream of Life* (New York: Farr, Straus, Giroux, 1999).

[6] I am grateful to Paul Heritage for drawing my attention to this point in the work of Tony Kushner.

[7] Recounted by Lluís Pasqual in Maria M. Delgado, "Redefining Spanish Theater: Lluís Pasqual on Directing, Fabià Puigserver and the Lliure," *Contemporary Theater Review*, vol. 7, part 4, 1998, p.101.

[8] *Viaje a la luna / Journey to the Moon* was first published in an English translation by Bernice G. Duncan in 1964 in *New Directions*, vol. 18, pp. 33–41. *Quimera* was first published in *Revista Hispánica Moderna*, vol. 6, nos 3–4, July-October 1940, pp. 312–313.

[9] Ed Morales, "Public Relations," *Village Voice*, 17–23 November 1998.

[10] Antonina Rodrigo, *Margarita Xirgu y su teatro* (Barcelona: Planeta, 1974), p. 168.

[11] Bonnie Marranca, *Ecologies of Theater: Essays at the Century Turning* (Baltimore: The John Hopkins University Press, 1996), p. 278.

[12] Pedro Alvarez Osorio, "*El público*," at "Lorca y la cultura árabe" conference, Gran Cairo Library, 10 November 1998.

Toward an Impossible Theater
An Introduction and Imagined Manifesto

By Caridad Svich

To begin, there must be space. In it, an image of yearning—the yearning to fill said space with one's soul. The soul is composed of signs and metaphors, symbols and lines. Odd disruptions are marked by time, which is incessant and not to be trusted. In the most innocent of objects lies malice. Trust nothing. Trust only heartbreak. Make theater out of that which is broken. Then take it apart again.

This is a naked theater, a poetic theater, a theater of the impossible, because it wishes to present on stage elements of the divine, the inexplicable, and the unnamed. "Call me a strange, hothouse flower, a freak, an ill-behaved child. I will not bend," this theater cries. Too much is at stake here: the fragile lives of spectral characters, the half-remembered songs of a time gone by, the static images made liquid by the force of memory. The impossible theater breaks with the folkloric and is unbound by the specifics of culture, and in so doing, is forever marked by the culture from which it springs.

What is Spanish here is everything: the emphasis on the lyric; the felicitous intrusion of low humor within the tragic or the refined; the inescapable, suffocating nostalgia for a time other than the present; and the coded behavior that restricts relationships and places them in the realm of the public even if what is happening is private. A personal iconography dominates the impossible theater, and demands that this iconography be read by an audience in an equally personal manner. The audience is positioned as decoder of the event being witnessed, not merely as spectator. Images are presented seemingly undigested—even if they have been carefully wrought. The irrational holds the key.

From the mountain
You could see her
Walking in bits
Like a horse
On wooden legs.

All alone at this hour
And no one looking
For the girl from Granada.

Talk is abolished. In its place is poetry or musical interchanges that owe as much to the world of commedia as avant-garde song. Phrases are repeated at intervals. Each time they are repeated, the meaning changes. The very repetition makes the audience and the characters question the meaning of what is being said. Characters in the impossible theater function as mutable fractals in a fickle universe over which they have little to no control. Fate overhangs, but it is not the fate of Greek drama, but rather a more cruel, less defined fate colored by Catholicism and inevitably marked by sacrifice.

The refuge that is found in this theater is the one offered by the free mixing of forms. Here are the flickering images and devices of the silent screen, where Buster Keaton's sad eyes are forever tormented by dreams. Images float by, midst a passing crowd or behind a lone individual framed in a torturous landscape. A jump cut can hurtle action forward or introduce a new character—an American Woman, a Clown, a forest of menacing trees—and the play moves without missing a beat. There is an embrace of the close-up, as interior states of character are revealed and time is suspended. There is also a profound use of the techniques of animation. In this theater, objects move and talk, mannequins weep and sing, and it is only natural, because in this theater human nature is not subject to corporate rationality. The lyrical impulse, which seeks transcendence, cannot be bought.

Let us look at a theater that embodies the theatrical. Here we have a stage that inhabits another stage, that mimics the conventions of another century to call attention to the one in which we are living. Clowns and harlequins from the world of the circus and commedia dell'arte interact with a Mask from the world of opera and melodrama. The cuckolded husband becomes the greatest of lovers, and puppets become spirits of strange, mythical benevolence. This is meta-theater written before the term was spoken. Part opera, part ritual, part comic strip, the impossible theater seeks a new form, a new voice to make itself heard. Excavating the past, this theater creates an eternal present where the future is glimpsed with eager, if furtive, eyes.

I give you an exquisite corpse. Pastiche, assemblage, and montage are delivered here in the body of the poet made martyr and celebrated in the cult of death that surrounds celebrity. Made up of old texts and new, and those yet to be written, this is queer theater for a non-queer age. Suffused with fear, trembling at its virility, impassioned at the very thought of love and its possibilities, the body thrashes in the bed of memory, and assembles out of it and its artifacts a text governed by the laws of synchronicity and simultaneity. Time is elastic, and thus is space. The corpse floats in full view of the audience, and begs for absolution, offering a singular, self-made beauty from its magpie purity.

He looks and looks
With sleepless eyes
And severed hands
For a boat on the sea

But what can he do
With these broken hands
That hold seven screams
Seven dreams
Seven blood streams
And fingers gnarled?

A night full of fish looks down
as the boy looks and looks.
But there is no moon, no boat
Only a cradle blue
in a silence without stars.

Perspectives shift. The body of the text and the poet turn full tilt as this theater looks to the future. The ghost of the impossible theater haunts the work of artists as diverse as Tennessee Williams, Sam Shepard, Matthew Bourne, and Robert Lepage. At home in the world of Cocteau and Dali, this theater is part of the spirit of art that seeks to break boundaries, and envision another way of not only making work but viewing it. To step into the impossible, you must leave preconceptions behind, but also bring them with you. The work demands that you understand deeply and with a profound sense of humor the traditions that are being called upon and how they are being dismantled and re-assembled. The perspectives that shift in the poetry of the pages of a cycle of poems born in New York are made to shift again in the plays made for the stage. The two-dimensional experiments are transported into the realm of the three-dimensional. Painting becomes installation.

Wounded love
Shot by the night's piercing stars
I want to see you
In the hollow mist,
In the shadow's fish
Mating with the broken dove.

I want to hold you
In my sunken womb
And let the green branches
Swallow my song.

Vision is sought, as in trying to capture a dream when waking. Sometimes the vision is lucid, sometimes obscure. An unconditional acceptance of the impossible is asked of the audience. After all, the experience of theater itself is chimerical. What is at heart here is an evocation of particular states of the human condition: A father leaves and an abandoned child cries, a husband kills himself in order to demonstrate the power of his love for his young wife, a maiden must choose between two lovers, and a young man lives in the timeless heartbreak engineered by an unrequited love and is ultimately undone by time.

The poet's visions play in the grooves of our mind long after the actual experience in the theater is over. What the impossible releases in its enactment is equivalent to the effect of an iconic close-up of a movie star in black-and-white: particles of light.

"I see you, I see you.
Let me hold you in my tongue.
Let me take you in my mouth unbled."

But no one saw
The girl from Granada
All alone at this hour

Walking down
On puppet legs

Only a boy in the window
a face between arms
a boy once known as Federico.

All poem excerpts are taken from *Ballads (After Lorca)* by Caridad Svich.

BUSTER KEATON
TAKES A WALK

El Paseo de Buster Keaton

A play by Federico García Lorca
in a new translation by Caridad Svich

ROOSTER: Cock-a-doodle-doo.

(Enter BUSTER KEATON with his four children by the hand.)

BUSTER KEATON: *(Draws a wooden knife and kills them.)* My poor little children.

ROOSTER: Cock-a-doodle-doo.

BUSTER KEATON: *(Counting the bodies on the ground.)* One, two, three, four.

(He mounts a bicycle and rides off. Among the old rubber tires and gasoline drums, a BLACK MAN eats his straw hat.)

BUSTER KEATON: What a lively afternoon!

(A parrot circles in the colorless sky.)

BUSTER KEATON: It's nice to ride around on a bicycle.

THE OWL: Whoo, whoo, whoo, who.

BUSTER KEATON: How well the little birds sing!

THE OWL: Whoooooooooooo.

BUSTER KEATON: It's quite moving.

(Pause. BUSTER KEATON crosses ineffably past the bulrushes and the small field of rye. The landscape grows smaller between the wheels of the machine. The bicycle is one-dimensional. It can fit inside books and lie flat in the bread oven. BUSTER KEATON's bicycle does not have a caramel seat and sugar pedals, as evil men would wish. It is a bicycle like any other, except it is soaked in innocence. Adam and Eve would run in fear if they saw a glass of water filled to the brim, but on the other hand, would caress KEATON's bicycle.)

BUSTER KEATON: Oh, love, love!

(BUSTER KEATON falls to the ground. The bicycle gets away. It escapes behind two large gray butterflies. He runs like crazy, half an inch off the ground.)

BUSTER KEATON: *(Rising.)* I have nothing to say. What can I say?

A VOICE: Idiot.

BUSTER KEATON: Very well.

(He walks on. His eyes, infinite and sad, like those of a newly born beast, dream of irises, angels, and silk belts. His eyes of rhinestone. His eyes of an idiot child. Which are so ugly. Which are so beautiful. His ostrich eyes. His human eyes in melancholy's steady equilibrium. In the distance, we see Philadelphia. The inhabitants of this urban city already know that the Singer machine's old poem can go back and forth among the large roses of the conservatories, although they will never understand that there is a subtle

poetic difference between a cup of hot tea and a cup of cold tea. In the distance, Philadelphia shines.)

BUSTER KEATON: This is a garden.

(An AMERICAN WOMAN with celluloid eyes appears out of the grass.)

AMERICAN WOMAN: Good afternoon.

(BUSTER KEATON smiles and looks lewdly at the woman's shoes. Oh, what shoes! Such shoes should not be allowed. You need the skin of three crocodiles to make them.)

BUSTER KEATON: I wish…

AMERICAN WOMAN: Have you a sword adorned with myrtle leaves?

(BUSTER KEATON shrugs and lifts his right foot.)

AMERICAN WOMAN: Have you a ring with a poisoned stone?

(BUSTER KEATON slowly closes his eyes and lifts his left foot.)

AMERICAN WOMAN: Well then?

(Four seraphim with sky-blue wings of gauze dance among the flowers. The young women of the city play the piano as if they were riding a bicycle. The waltz, the moon, and the canoes break our friend's dear heart. To everyone's great surprise, Autumn has invaded the garden, like water in a geometrical sugar lump.)

BUSTER KEATON: *(Sighing.)* I wish I were a swan. But I cannot be it, even though I wish. Because, where would I leave my hat? Where, my wing collar and moiré tie? Such misfortune!

(A YOUNG WOMAN, wasp-waisted and with a high topknot, passes by, riding a bicycle. She has the head of a nightingale.)

YOUNG WOMAN: Whom do I have the honor of addressing?

BUSTER KEATON: *(Bowing.)* Buster Keaton.

(The YOUNG WOMAN faints and falls from her bicycle. Her striped legs tremble on the grass like two dying zebras. A gramophone plays in a thousand shows at the same time: "There are nightingales in America.")

BUSTER KEATON: *(Kneeling.)* Miss Eleanor, forgive me, it wasn't me! Miss! *(Softly.)* Miss! *(Softer now.)* Miss!

(He kisses her.)

(The brilliant star of the police gleams on Philadelphia's horizon.)

Marjorie Ballentine as The Wife
from *Chimera*
The Drama League, New York, New York, 1989

photo by Caridad Svich

CHIMERA

Quimera

A play by Federico García Lorca
in a new translation by Caridad Svich

This play was presented as part of
The Drama League of New York's "Directors Project, 1989"
December 7–10, 1989, at Circle Rep Studio.

Director: Beth Schachter
Set Design: Dan Conway, Costume Design: Michael Krass
Light Design: Brian McDevitt, Sound Design: John Bowen

With cast as follows:

Old Man . . . . Divina Cook
Young Girl . . . . Monique Cintron
The Wife . . . . Marjorie Ballentine
Henry . . . . Mark Tymchyshyn

(Door.)

HENRY: Good-bye.

SIX VOICES: *(From inside.)* Good-bye.

HENRY: I'll be staying in the mountains a long time.

VOICE: A squirrel.

HENRY: Yes, a squirrel for you, and five birds, five birds that no child has ever seen before.

VOICE: No, I want a lizard.

VOICE: And I a mole.

HENRY: You're all very different, children. I will do as each of you says.

OLD MAN: Very different.

HENRY: What did you say?

OLD MAN: May I take your bags?

HENRY: No.

(Children's laughter is heard.)

OLD MAN: Are they your children?

HENRY: All six of them.

OLD MAN: I've known their mother for a long time. Your wife. I was your driver for a while, but if I must confess, I'm better off now, as a beggar. The horses. Ha! Nobody knows how frightened I am of horses! May lightning fall over all of their eyes. Guiding a carriage is very difficult. Oh! Extremely difficult. If you're not afraid, you don't find out, and if you find out, you're not afraid. Damned be the horses!

HENRY: *(Taking the bags.)* Let me.

OLD MAN: No, No. I'll take them, for some little coins, the smallest you have, I'll take them for you. Your wife will thank you for it. She wasn't afraid of the horses. She is happy.

HENRY: Let's go soon. At six I must take the train.

OLD MAN: Ah, the train! That's a different matter. The train is nonsense. Even if I live to be a hundred, I'll never be afraid of the train. The train isn't alive. It goes by and has gone by… But the horses… Look.

WIFE: *(At the window.)* Henry, my love. Henry. Don't forget to write. Don't forget me.

OLD MAN: Ah, the young girl! *(Laughs.)* Do you remember how he would leap over the mud wall, how he would climb up the trees only so he could see you?

WIFE: I'll remember it until the day I die.

HENRY: Me, too.

WIFE: I'll wait for you. Good-bye.

HENRY: Good-bye.

OLD MAN: Don't worry yourself. She's yours. She loves you. You love her. Don't worry.

HENRY: It's true, but this loss weighs heavy on me.

OLD MAN: Could be worse. Worse is that everything goes on, that the river keeps on running. Worse is if a cyclone would hit.

HENRY: I'm not in the mood for jokes. You're always like this.

OLD MAN: Ha! Everyone else in the world…but you're the first to believe that what's important about a cyclone is the destruction it causes, and I believe all the contrary. What's important about a cyclone…

HENRY: *(Getting aggravated.)* Come on. It'll be six at any moment.

OLD MAN: And what of the sea?… In the sea…

HENRY: *(Furiously.)* Let's go, I said.

OLD MAN: Aren't you forgetting anything?

HENRY: I leave everything perfectly in order. And besides, what's it to you? The worst thing in the world is an old servant, a beggar.

VOICE #1: Daddy.

VOICE #2: Daddy.

VOICE #3: Daddy.

VOICE #4: Daddy.

VOICE #5: Daddy.

VOICE #6: Daddy.

OLD MAN: Your children.

HENRY: My children.

GIRL: *(At the door.)* I don't want the squirrel. If you bring me the squirrel, I won't love you. Don't bring me the squirrel. I don't want it.

VOICE: Nor I the lizard.

VOICE: Nor I the mole.

GIRL: We want you to bring us a set of minerals.

VOICE: No, no, I want my mole.

VOICE: No, the mole is for me.

(Quarrel.)

GIRL: *(Entering.)* Well, now the mole will be for me.

HENRY: Enough! Now be happy.

OLD MAN: You said they were all different.

HENRY: Yes, very different. Fortunately.

OLD MAN: What?

HENRY: *(Forcefully.)* Fortunately.

OLD MAN: *(Sadly.)* Fortunately.

(They exit.)

WIFE: *(At the window.)* Good-bye.

VOICE: Good-bye.

WIFE: Come back soon.

VOICE: *(In the distance.)* Soon.

WIFE: He will bundle up well at night. He takes four blankets. I, in turn, will be alone in bed. I will be cold. He has marvelous eyes; but what I love is his strength. *(She undresses.)* My back hurts a bit. Ah! If he could despise me! I want him to despise me… and to love me. I want to run away and have him catch me. I want him to burn me…to burn me… *(Loudly.)* Good-bye, good-bye…Henry. Henry… I love you. I see you. You are small now. You jump over the stones. Small. Now I could swallow you, as if you were a button. I could swallow you. Henry…

GIRL: Mommy.

WIFE: Don't go out. A cold wind has come up. I said no!

(Enters. Light fades.)

GIRL: *(Quickly.)* Daddyyy! Daddyyy! Bring me the squirrel. I don't want the minerals. Minerals break my nails. Daddyyy!

BOY: *(At the door.)* He-doesn't-hear you. He-doesn't-hear-you. He-doesn't-hear you.

GIRL: Daddy, but I want the squirrel. *(Bursting into tears.)* Dear God! I want the squirrel!

THE MAIDEN, THE SAILOR, AND THE STUDENT

La doncella, el marinero, y el estudiante

A play by Federico García Lorca
in a new translation by Caridad Svich

Monique Cintron as Young Girl and Marjorie Ballentine as The Wife
from *Chimera*
The Drama League, New York, New York, 1989

photo by Caridad Svich

(Balcony.)

OLD WOMAN: *(On the street.)* Snaiiiiils! Cook them in saffron, mint, and bay leaves.

MAIDEN: Little snails from the country. They look like an ancient Chinese city all bunched up in the basket.

OLD WOMAN: This old woman is selling them. They are big and dark. Four of them could kill a snake. What snails! My God, what snails!

MAIDEN: Let me embroider. My pillows have no monograms and it scares me…Because, is there a young girl in the world that doesn't have her clothes marked?

OLD WOMAN: What are your initials?

MAIDEN: I stitch the whole alphabet onto my clothes.

OLD WOMAN: What for?

MAIDEN: So that the man who is with me can call me whatever he desires.

OLD WOMAN: *(Sadly.)* Then you're a tramp.

MAIDEN: *(Lowering her eyes.)* Yes.

OLD WOMAN: You'll call yourself Mary, Rose, Trinidad? Segismunda?

MAIDEN: And more, and more.

OLD WOMAN: Eustaquia? Dorothy? Jenny?

MAIDEN: And more, more, more…

(The MAIDEN raises the palms of her hands, grown pale from the sleeplessness of the silk and the samplers. The OLD WOMAN runs away, seeking the wall's protection, toward her Siberia of dark rags, where the basket full of breadcrusts is dying.)

MAIDEN: A, B, C, D, E, F, G, H, I, J, K, L, M, N. That's enough for now. I'll close the balcony. I'll sit behind the windows and continue my stitching.

MOTHER: *(Off.)* Daughter, daughter, are you crying?

MAIDEN: No. It's starting to rain.

(A motorboat adorned with blue flags crosses the bay, leaving a stuttering song in its wake. The rain crowns the city with a Doctor of Letters cap. In the bars by the port the great merry-go-round of drunken sailors begins.)

MAIDEN: *(Singing.)* A, B, C, D.
Which letter is for me?
Sailor begins with S-A
Student begins with S-T,
A, B, C, D.

SAILOR: *(Entering.)* Me.

MAIDEN: You.

SAILOR: *(Sadly.)* A boat isn't much of anything.

MAIDEN: I'll deck it with flags and sweets.

SAILOR: If the captain agrees.

    (Pause.)

MAIDEN: *(Distressed.)* A boat isn't much of anything!

SAILOR: I'll fill it with lace embroidery.

MAIDEN: If my mother lets me.

SAILOR: Stand up.

MAIDEN: What for?

SAILOR: So I can see you.

MAIDEN: *(Rises.)* Here I am.

SAILOR: What lovely thighs you have!

MAIDEN: I rode a bicycle when I was a child.

SAILOR: And I, a dolphin.

MAIDEN: You're lovely, too.

SAILOR: When I'm nude.

MAIDEN: What do you know how to do?

SAILOR: Stroke.

    (The SAILOR plays the accordion, which is as dusty and tired as the seventeenth century.)

STUDENT: *(Entering.)* It's going too fast.

MAIDEN: Who's going too fast?

STUDENT: The century.

MAIDEN: You're confused.

STUDENT: I'm running, you see.

MAIDEN: From whom?

STUDENT: From the coming year.

MAIDEN: Have you not seen my face?

STUDENT: That's why I've stopped.

MAIDEN: You haven't a tan.

STUDENT: I live at night, you see.

MAIDEN: What do you want?

STUDENT: Give me water.

MAIDEN: We haven't a well.

STUDENT: Well, I'm dying of thirst!

MAIDEN: I'll give you milk from my breasts.

STUDENT: *(Ardent.)* Sweeten my mouth.

MAIDEN: But I'm a maiden.

STUDENT: If you drop me a ladder, I'll spend this night with you.

MAIDEN: You're white and you'll be very cold.

STUDENT: My arms are very strong.

MAIDEN: I'll let you if my mother agrees to it.

STUDENT: Go on.

MAIDEN: No.

STUDENT: And why not?

MAIDEN: Well because I don't…

STUDENT: Come on…

MAIDEN: No.

(A circle of dark vessels revolves around the moon. Three sirens splashing in the waves deceive the coast-guards on the cliff. The MAIDEN, on her balcony, considers jumping off the letter Z and throwing herself into the abyss. EMILIO PRADOS and MANOLITO ALTOLAGUIRRE*, as white as flour from their fear of the sea, carry her gently away from the railing.)

END OF PLAY

* *Note: Poets Emilio Prados and Manolito Altolaguirre ran a small press and published García Lorca's SONGS.*

BICYCLES, FISHES, AND CELLULOID EYES:
AVANT-GARDE STRAINS IN LORCA'S WORK

By Sarah Wright

In 1925 Lorca worked simultaneously on his play *Amor de Don Perlimplín con Belisa en su jardín* (*The Love of Don Perlimplín for Belisa in His Garden*) and a series of highly experimental short prose pieces, which he described as "pure poetry. Naked."[1] Amongst these avant-garde "dialogues" were *El paseo de Buster Keaton* (*Buster Keaton Takes a Walk*), *La doncella, el marinero y estudiante* (*The Maiden, The Sailor, and The Student*) and *Quimera* (*Chimera*). A *chimera* is a nightmarish dream or imagined reality, and in a sense all three "dialogues" seem to take place in a strange, liminal realm between wakefulness and sleep. *El paseo de Buster Keaton* (*Buster Keaton Takes a Walk*) is neither play nor film-script: The author's long, lyrical stage directions (which include a close-up) are pure poetry and often seem as if they would be difficult to translate into cinema: "To everyone's great surprise, Autumn has invaded the garden, like water in a geometrical sugar lump." With this piece Lorca was exploring cinematic vision rather than using the language of cinema itself. But at the same time, the dialogue is sparse in the manner of captions of the silent screen, and the piece as a whole appears filtered through cinematic references. The American Woman has "celluloid eyes," whilst the striped legs of the Young Woman, as she falls from her bicycle, "tremble on the grass like two dying zebras," reminiscent of the flickering strobe effect of early cinema. The protagonist, Buster Keaton, is as doleful as his cinematic alter-ego ("his eyes, infinite and sad, like those of a newly born beast"), yet in this surrealist plot his slapstick extends to drawing a wooden knife and killing his four children before impassively counting their bodies ("one, two, three, four").[2] But Buster is still the innocent in a difficult urban world, where automata (Singer sewing machines and gramophones) threaten delicacy, individuality, and intuition:

> the inhabitants of this urban city already know that
> the Singer machine's old poem can go back and forth
> among the large roses of the conservatories, although
> they will never understand that there is a subtle poet-
> ic difference between a cup of hot tea and a cup of
> cold tea.

Buster dreams of escaping the constraints of his world: "I wish I were a swan. But I cannot be it, even though I wish." But this poignant moment is undercut as he continues, "because, where would I leave my hat? Where, my wing collar and moiré tie? Such misfortune!" The piece ends with a cinematic kiss followed by a fade to a long shot of the police cars arriving from the fake distant horizon of Philadelphia.

La doncella, el marinero y el estudiante (*The Maiden, The Sailor, and the Student*) is a compact yet fluid game of words and images. The Maiden declares that she will embroider the whole alphabet onto her trousseau, "so that the man who is with me can call me whatever he desires." She is nothing more than a blank page for a man to write on. In a series of beautifully condensed images, the Sailor arrives, with an accordion that is as dusty and tired as the seventeenth-century, whilst the Student is in constant flight from the coming year. Sexual desire reverberates in this piece, but the relationships between the Maiden and her suitors are doomed: Finally, "the Maiden, on her balcony, considers jumping off the letter Z and throwing herself into the abyss," before being gently led away.

Quimera (*Chimera*) deals wistfully with a father's farewell to his family. In the wake of startling new inventions, travel was a great preoccupation of the early years of the twentieth century. Here, Henry, the traveller, is preoccupied with the time ("at six I must take the train"), whilst his children clamor for his attention. After the traveller leaves, he becomes no more than a fading voice and a small figure in the distance, no larger than a button. The play deals with high emotions experienced in the face of the cruel indifference that is absence: The wife rails against the anticipated stony-faced loneliness ("I want him to despise me... and to love me"), whilst the little girl issues her distraught request for her father's attention into the silent darkness.

Amor de Don Perlimplín con Belisa en su jardín (*The Love of Don Perlimplín for Belisa in his Garden*, 1926) is subtitled "erotic alleluia" and deals with the marriage of an old man (Don Perlimplín) to a young bride (Belisa). An alleluia was a nineteenth-century vignette, which often featured the cradle-to-grave story of the stock figure Don Perlimplín.[3] Lorca wrote of this piece that with it he intended to blend the lyrical and the grotesque, and whilst the characters are derived from farce, the plot is very dark.[4] The marriage between Perlimplín and Belisa is engineered by an interfering maid named Marcolfa. Belisa's mother, who is dressed in a glorious wig full of birds, ribbons, and glass beads, goes along with Marcolfa's plotting out of her desire for financial gain. Belisa is young, beautiful, and powerfully erotic: "Love, love./ Between my concealed thighs/ swims like a fish the sun." The pair marry, but whilst Perlimplín's sexual awakening is symbolized by his growing thirst, he is also terrified of Belisa: "When I was a child a woman strangled her husband. He was a shoemaker. I can't forget it. I always thought not to marry. With my books, I have enough." The implication is that their marriage is never consummated, and what is more, on the morning after their wedding night, Perlimplín awakes to find "enormous horns, golden and blossoming, on his head": the symbol of cuckoldry. After being told by Marcolfa that five men entered his bedchamber while he was sleeping, he is determined to win Belisa's heart, and her imagination. He invents a fantastical young man in a red cape to seduce her. Belisa never quite manages to see this mysterious lover: He is always teasingly disappearing around corners with his red cape swirling around him. But she imagines him: "He must be dark and his kisses must perfume and burn like saffron and clove. Sometimes he walks below my balconies and waves his hand slowly in a greeting that makes my breasts tremble." Perlimplín's plot is as dangerous as it is ingenious, for he has managed to enter Belisa's imagination, to fill her head with the anticipation of a lover so wonderful that she could never love anyone else. He believes that he has taught her the meaning of a love divorced from carnal desire, a love of the soul and the spirit. In a cunning reworking of the honor-code, Perlimplín decides to kill his wife's lover (and with that act, himself). At the same time he declares that he must kill himself to teach Belisa about the nature of love. He stabs himself. But although Belisa realizes that it is not her lover beneath the cape but her husband Perlimplín, she seems not to understand that Perlimplín was the fantasy lover all-along: "But where is the young man with the red cape? Dear God, where is he?" Belisa will therefore search endlessly for her lost love, in a state of perpetual unrequited love—she seems, therefore, to have understood little of Perlimplín's convoluted aims. The last speech is given over to Marcolfa, who has been an ambiguous figure throughout and leaves us wondering about her motives in the plot. Her words seem to suggest that Perlimplín's intention was not martyrdom for Belisa's sake, as he has ostentatiously maintained, but rather revenge: "Don Perlimplín, sleep in peace... Do you hear her? Don Perlimplín... do you hear her?" The final twist is that almost the whole play may have taken place within Perlimplín's imagination, precipitated by the fear he experienced in anticipation of marriage to Belisa. The play is unsettling in its resistance to neat classifications and troubling in its insinuation of rumor and plot happening somewhere beneath the surface of the text.

If *Amor de Don Perlimplín con Belisa en su jardín* (*The Love of Don Perlimplín for Belisa in the Garden*) deals with projected fantasies and tantalizing anticipation, then the same is true of *Así que pasen cinco años* (*As Five Years Pass,* 1931). This play depicts a staggered and mismatched heterosexual desire: The Young Man is betrothed to his Fiancée, but he cannot marry her until five years have passed. He stoically enjoys this situation, however, as the image he carries of her in his imagination is more alive for him than any reality: "I needed to keep my distance from her so I could focus on her, yes, that is the word, focus her in my heart." After five years have passed, however, his betrothed has fallen in love with the Rugby Player, who never speaks, but smokes silently while she projects her fantasies onto him. And when the Typist subsequently declares her love for the Young Man, he decrees that they wait another five years: Consummation is endlessly deferred. The play is the articulation of a perpetual passionate yearning, where characters project fantasies onto one another against a backdrop of the decay of modern urban life.

What all of these works have in common is that although often slight in length, they offer a tantalizing glimpse of characters whose potential relationships weigh far more heavily than their actual relations with others. The pieces shimmer with highly visual, cinematic references, and present a string of often disjointed yet mesmerizing imagistic and linguistic juxtapositions that create often unexpectedly strong emotional connections.

---

[1] See letters to Melchor Fernández Almagro in *Epistolario Completo*, eds. A.A. Anderson and C. Maurer, Madrid: Cátedra, 1997, pp. 283–4, 300.

[2] The piece seems reminiscent of Keaton's *Sherlock Jr.* (1924), in which Keaton, a cinema projectionist, falls asleep at work; a dream-sequence follows in which Keaton is transposed into a series of absurdly changing backdrops.

[3] Helen Grant recuperates popular vignettes featuring Don Perlimplín in her article, "Una aleluya erótica de Federico García Lorca y las aleluyas populares del siglo XIX," *Actas del Primer Congreso Internacional de Hispanistas*, Oxford: Dolphin Books, 1964, pp. 307–314 and Margarita Ucelay explores the same theme in her excellent companion piece to the play, *Amor de Don Perlimplín con Belisa en su jardín*, Madrid: Cátedra, 1990.

[4] See Federico García Lorca, *Obras Completas*, III, Arturo del Hoyo, ed., Madrid: Aguilar, 1986, p.521.

LORCA'S *THE LOVE OF DON PERLIMPLÍN FOR BELISA IN THE GARDEN:*
THE PERSPECTIVES ARE DELICIOUSLY WRONG

Jim Carmody
University of California–San Diego

The introductions to two recent books on Federico García Lorca offer perspectives on the playwright and on the study of his work that help map the significance of Caridad Svich's new translations of several plays and selections from *Poet in New York*. Paul Smith opens his *The Theater of García Lorca* (Cambridge University Press, 1998) with accounts of the move of the Fundación Federico García Lorca to its new location in Madrid in 1994 and the opening of a museum near Granada in 1995. For Smith, these events mark "the definitive institutionalization of García Lorca in Spain, the poet's consolidation as an academic and a popular icon..." (p.1). Where Smith begins by pointing to the consolidation of Lorca's status in Spanish culture, C. Christopher Soufas opens his *Audience and Authority in the Modernist Theater of Federico García Lorca* (University of Alabama Press, 1996) by pointing to the "continuing lack of consensus about the theater of Federico García Lorca..." (p.1). That Lorca has achieved the iconic cultural status described by Smith in the absence of a critical, interpretive consensus can be attributed in part to the fact that the Lorca canon itself continues to evolve, with a new version of the *Obras completas* published in 1986, in part to the fact that major plays have received their first performances decades after the artist's death (notably the famous Lluís Pasqual staging of *El público*, which was first performed at the Piccolo Teatro in Milan in 1986), and in part to the rapid evolution of theory and its influence on cultural, literary, and theater studies. Indeed, the two books by Smith and Soufas are both products of such a simultaneous interest in both Lorca and theory.

To these perspectives that point simultaneously to García Lorca's status as a cultural icon and to the contested nature of his identity as the creator of objects of culture (what Barthes and Foucault would have called an Author) must be added the perspective of American and British theater historians. Oscar Brockett, widely regarded as the leading American theater historian of the last fifty years or so, grants Lorca one and a half short paragraphs in the most recent edition of his *History of the Theater* (Allyn & Bacon, 1999). Brockett mentions none of the texts translated by Caridad Svich and concludes by saying that *Blood Wedding, Yerma,* and *The House of Bernarda Alba,* which he calls the "major plays," "[b]lending poetic imagery with primitive passions…are usually considered the finest Spanish works since the Golden Age" (p. 479). Christopher Innes, who contributed the "Theater After Two World Wars" chapter to John Russell Brown's *Oxford Illustrated History of Theater* (Oxford University Press, 1995) mentions only *Blood Wedding* and *Yerma* (p. 410). Innes' brief discussion of Lorca is, however, considerably more informative than Brockett's. He tells us that Lorca was a close friend of Dali and Buñuel, and he describes his dramaturgy as a combination of "a surrealist approach with traditional subjects." Most usefully, he calls attention to Lorca's "distinctively modernist physical poetry, combining lyrical language with carefully orchestrated light, colour, and music." Like Brockett, Innes mentions none of the texts translated by Caridad Svich.

If one were to map Svich's translations with respect to the perspectives outlined above, one would have to conclude that she has worked with texts that are not yet on the Anglo-American theater-historical map and that her work can be seen as further complicating the tasks of institutionalizing Lorca as cultural icon and achieving a consensus with respect to the interpretation of his work. Svich's translations produce such a complication because she has elected to translate none of the so-called major plays, the canonical trio of rural tragedies of "poetic imagery and primitive passions." Instead, Svich has selected a range of texts that emphasize the diversity of Lorca's writing. The Lorca we encounter reading texts as different from one another as *Buster Keaton Takes a Walk, The Love of Don Perlimplín for Belisa in the Garden, As Five Years Pass,* and *Poet in New York* is not the same Lorca we meet reading *Blood Wedding* or *The House of Bernarda Alba.* Indeed, we encounter a very different Lorca in all of the plays and poems, an experience that will continue to surprise us only as long as we retain our culturally conditioned acceptance of the critical notion that an author's work forms a unified whole and that we will arrive at a more perfect interpretation of an author's work once we have understood exactly the ways in which a given author's work forms such a unified whole. In the case of Federico García Lorca, that work was both abundant and exceptionally varied, despite his assassination at a relatively early age, and it was not restricted to the medium of writing alone. In addition to writing for the stage, Lorca worked as an actor and director; he also wrote a short film script. Quite apart from the written word, Lorca was an accomplished musician and graphic artist. Looking at Lorca's work from the end of the twentieth century, looking at Lorca's work from a perspective formed by encounters with postmodernism and poststructuralism, with all they have taught us about the "death of the author" and the endlessly shifting nature of identity, we can only rejoice that we have so much of Lorca's work, so many different Lorcas to encounter.

While no single work represents the "real" Lorca, Caridad Svich's translations bring several different Lorcas to our attention, and while each of these texts provides ample evidence of the theatrical richness of Lorca's imagination, each one must be taken on its own terms. *The Love of Don Perlimplín for Belisa in the Garden*, subtitled "an erotic alleluia in four frames," manages to compact a great deal of dramatic material and technique into its short duration. The title itself points to the nature of some of this complexity and hints at how we might read the play. In the title, Lorca combines the elements of a romantic comedy ("love," "Don Perlimplín," "Belisa," "garden") with a graphic narrative format for children (alleluia) that is paradoxically labeled "erotic." Lorca thus draws our attention to the traditional elements of character and plot while foregrounding the manner in which he has chosen to combine them. If the elements themselves seem traditional, even old-fashioned (the alleluia was at the time already an old-fashioned form although not as ancient as the dramatic narrative it promised to contain), the way in which Lorca combines them seems strikingly modern. Indeed, the strategic combination of elements frankly presented as old-fashioned marks virtually every moment of the play, constantly asking us to divide our attention between the scene performed on stage and Lorca's way of framing the scene for us.

Here again, the title offers another hint with respect to Lorca's dramaturgical intentions. Rather than promise a play in four scenes, Lorca's subtitle offers "four frames," although even a cursory reading of the play will raise the frame count considerably higher as each scene or frame introduces a greater number and complexity of frames and framings. The frames are literally embodied in the many doors and windows represented on stage and metaphorically enacted in both the language spoken by the characters and the dramatic motifs themselves. Finally, to all the frames on stage we can add the title itself, which names both the text on whose cover it appears and the performance on stage. Lorca's description of Don Perlimplín's dining room in Frame Three provides an apt description of the puzzle adroitly constructed by Lorca for readers and for theater artists who choose to stage this play: "The perspectives are deliciously wrong."

What matters with perspective, of course, is the position of the spectator, and one of the many delights of the plays is the many ways in which Lorca manages to frame spectating as a dramatic activity, for each of the characters is, at times, as much a spectator as any of us in the audience. Like the characters in this world of deliciously wrong perspectives, we too engage in the task of trying to understand our role, a task that Lorca complicates by continually shifting the genre of the scene. As a scene veers from the farcical to the pathetic, employing tones that range from the prosaic to the sublime, like the actors, we constantly seek to find our bearings. Is this moment supposed to be so comic? Is that moment really supposed to be so lyrical? The more we seek a neoclassical unity, the more this heterogeneous dramaturgy eludes us.

And yet if we stop seeking a stable vantage point from which all events come into a recognizable perspective, and if we stop trying to arrest the constant shifting of the frame, and enter into the flow of images and events, we find in this fragmented, destabilized, dramatic world moments of extraordinary emotional resonance and human understanding, all the more startling because Lorca's dramaturgy has managed to separate them from the kind of dramatic framework we might normally have expected to contain them. Framing and re-framing his images, employing montage rather than plot, Lorca in this play creates fresh and startling theatrical images out of the outdated cultural codes of earlier periods.

Andy Weems as Don Perlimplín and Maggie Stewart as Belisa
in *The Love of Don Perlimplín for Belisa in the Garden*
University of California—San Diego

photo from the University of California—San Diego photo archives

THE LOVE OF DON PERLIMPLÍN FOR BELISA IN THE GARDEN

Amor de Don Perlimplín con Belisa en su Jardín

An erotic alleluia in four frames by Federico García Lorca
in a new translation by Caridad Svich

This play was presented at
The University of California—San Diego
MFA Department of Theater's Imagine Series
November 30–December 4, 1988.

Director: Maria Joy Mileaf
Set Design: Tom Mays, Costume Design: Mary Larson
Light Design: Brenda Berry, Sound Design: Victor Zupanc
Puppet Design: Brenda Berry, Dramaturgy: Caridad Svich

With cast as follows

Don Perlimplín . . . . Andy Weems
Belisa . . . . Maggie Stewart
Marcolfa . . . . Tom Nelis
Mother . . . . Karen Vesper

TRANSLATOR'S NOTE:

Alleluia—
1. Praise be to God.
2. Eighteenth century Spanish equivalent of comic strips.

Oddly beautiful, playful, ironic, and savage, *The Love of Don Perlimplín for Belisa in the Garden* is a play that like García Lorca's more famous works *Blood Wedding* and *Yerma* springs from "duende," word and concept of flamenco that became the artistic touchstone for the Spanish playwright and poet.

"Duende" is a power or demon that cannot be summoned at will, but when it arrives its force is irresistible, for it is what drives a creation. What makes a dancer, for example, seem possessed by a baptismal fire of the soul. The demon is also the source of laughter, and in Lorca, it is the black laughter of one who confronts death and then decides to joke with it, albeit briefly. Like the work of his fellow countrymen Luis Buñuel and Salvador Dalí, Lorca's characters tiptoe between comedy and tragedy, the two theatrical masks. What results from this tiptoe is heartbreak—human, theatrical, and very much alive. Religion, social class, gender roles, morality: Forms frame his characters. What is left for them to do, then, but desire?

And so, on the delectable but profound surface we remain, seeing things not as they are, but as we are.

Caridad Svich

FRAME ONE

(Don Perlimplín's house. Green walls, with chairs and furniture painted black. In the background, a balcony from which Belisa's balcony can be seen. A sonata is heard. PERLIMPLÍN wears a green dress-coat and white wig full of ringlets; MARCOLFA, his servant, wears the classic striped garb.)

PERLIMPLÍN: Yes?

MARCOLFA: Yes.

PERLIMPLÍN: But, why yes?

MARCOLFA: Because it's yes.

PERLIMPLÍN: And if I told you no?

MARCOLFA: *(Sourly.)* Why no?

PERLIMPLÍN: No.

MARCOLFA: Tell me, my dear sir, the reasons for this "no."

PERLIMPLÍN: You tell me, persevering domestic, your reasons for this "yes."

(Pause.)

MARCOLFA: Twenty and twenty are forty…

PERLIMPLÍN: *(Listening.)* Go on.

MARCOLFA: And ten, fifty.

PERLIMPLÍN: Come on.

MARCOLFA: With fifty years now you are not a child.

PERLIMPLÍN: Exactly.

MARCOLFA: I could die at any moment.

PERLIMPLÍN: Exactly!

MARCOLFA: *(Crying.)* And what will become of you alone in this world?

PERLIMPLÍN: What would be.

MARCOLFA: That's why you must marry.

PERLIMPLÍN: *(Distracted.)* Yes?

MARCOLFA: *(With vigor.)* Yes.

PERLIMPLÍN: *(Anguished.)* But, Marcolfa… Why yes? When I was a child a woman strangled her husband. He was a shoemaker. I can't forget it. I've always thought not to marry. With my books, I have enough. What good will it do?

MARCOLFA: The marriage contract has great charms, my lord. It's not what you see from outside. It's full of hidden things. Things that aren't proper for a maid to say… You see…

PERLIMPLÍN: What's wrong?

MARCOLFA: I'm blushing.

(Pause. A piano is heard.)

BELISA'S VOICE: *(From off, singing.)*

Love, love.

Between my concealed thighs

swims like a fish the sun.

Warm water between the rushes,

love.

Cock, quickly the night is going!

Don't let it go, no!

MARCOLFA: My lord will see how right I am.

PERLIMPLÍN: *(Scratching his head.)* Sings well.

MARCOLFA: That's the woman for my lord: the pure Belisa.

PERLIMPLÍN: Belisa… but wouldn't it be better…

MARCOLFA: No… Come along right now.

(She takes him by the hand and they approach the balcony.)

MARCOLFA: You must say "Belisa."

PERLIMPLÍN: Belisa.

MARCOLFA: Louder.

PERLIMPLÍN: Belisa!

(The balcony of the house across the street opens and BELISA appears, resplendent in her beauty. She is half-naked.)

BELISA: Who calls?

(MARCOLFA hides behind the balcony's curtain.)

MARCOLFA: Answer!

PERLIMPLÍN: *(Trembling.)* It was I calling.

BELISA: Yes?

PERLIMPLÍN: Yes.

BELISA: But… why yes?

PERLIMPLÍN: Because it's yes.

BELISA: And if I told you no?

PERLIMPLÍN: I'd be hurt… because… we have decided that I want to marry.

BELISA: *(Laughs.)* With whom?

PERLIMPLÍN: With you.

BELISA: *(Serious.)* But… *(Shouting.)* Mom, mom, mommy!

MARCOLFA: This goes well.

(Her MOTHER appears with a grand eighteenth-century wig full of birds, ribbons, and glass beads.)

BELISA: Don Perlimplín wants to marry me. What do I do?

MOTHER: Good good afternoon, enchanting little neighbor of mine. I always told my poor daughter that you had the charm and manners of that great woman who was once your mother, whom I never had the good fortune to meet.

PERLIMPLÍN: I'm charmed.

MARCOLFA: *(Furious, from behind the curtain.)* I have decided we're going…

MOTHER: To take up marriage, am I right?

PERLIMPLÍN: That's right.

BELISA: But mom… And me?

MOTHER: You're agreed, naturally. Don Perlimplín is an enchanting husband.

PERLIMPLÍN: I hope to be, madam.

MARCOLFA: *(Calling DON PERLIMPLÍN.)* This is almost done.

PERLIMPLÍN: You think…?

(They talk.)

MOTHER: *(To BELISA.)* Don Perlimplín has a lot of land; on the lands are many geese and sheep. The sheep are taken to the market. In the market, people pay money for them. Money brings beauty… And beauty is valued by all the other men.

BELISA: Then…

MOTHER: You are greatly moved… Belisa… go inside… it's not proper for a maiden to have certain conversations.

BELISA: 'Til later…

(She leaves.)

MOTHER: She is a lily. You see her face? *(Lowering her voice.)* Well, if you saw her… Like sugar… But…sorry. I shouldn't broach these things with a person as modest and supremely competent as you…

PERLIMPLÍN: Yes?

MOTHER: Yes…I have said it without irony.

PERLIMPLÍN: I don't know how to express our gratitude.

MOTHER: Oh, our gratitude! …what extraordinary delicacy! The gratitude of your heart and yours as well… I have understood… despite the fact that it has been twenty years since I have dealt with a man.

MARCOLFA: *(Aside.)* The wedding.

PERLIMPLÍN: The wedding…

MOTHER: Whenever you'd like… although *(Produces handkerchief and cries.)* to all mothers… 'til later.

(She exits.)

MARCOLFA: Finally.

PERLIMPLÍN: Oh, Marcolfa, Marcolfa! Into what world are you going to plunge me?

MARCOLFA: Into the world of matrimony.

PERLIMPLÍN: And if I'm frank with you… I feel a thirst… Why don't you bring me water?

(MARCOLFA draws closer, whispers in his ear.)

PERLIMPLÍN: Who would believe it?

(Piano is heard. Theater in half-light. BELISA draws the curtains of her balcony, nearly nude, singing languidly.)

BELISA: Love, love.

Between my concealed thighs

Swims like a fish the sun.

MARCOLFA: Beautiful maiden.

PERLIMPLÍN: Like sugar… white on the inside. Will she be capable of strangling me?

MARCOLFA: A woman grows weak if you scare her in time.

BELISA: Love…

Cock, the night is going!

PERLIMPLÍN: What is she saying, Marcolfa? What is she saying?

(MARCOLFA laughs.)

PERLIMPLÍN: And what is this coming over me? What is this?

(Piano continues. Past the balcony, a flock of black paper birds go by as SCENE CHANGE.)

Duende #1 and Duende #2 puppets, designed by Brenda Berry
from *The Love of Don Perlimplín for Belisa in the Garden*
University of California—San Diego, 1988

photo from U.C.S.D. Theater archives

FRAME TWO

Don Perlimplín's bedchamber. In the center, a grand bed with a canopy and a crest of feathers. On the walls are six doors. The first on the right serves as entrance and exit for DON PERLIMPLÍN. It is the wedding night. MAR-COLFA enters with candelabrum in hand, from the first door on the left.

MARCOLFA: Good evening.

BELISA'S VOICE: *(From off.)* Good-bye, Marcolfa.

(PERLIMPLÍN appears, dressed magnificently.)

MARCOLFA: Have a good wedding night, my master.

PERLIMPLÍN: Good-bye, Marcolfa.

(MARCOLFA exits. PERLIMPLÍN tiptoes toward the room in front and looks from the door.)

PERLIMPLÍN: Belisa, with so much lace, you look like a wave, and you give me the same fear that as a child I had of the ocean. Ever since you arrived from the church, my house is full of secret rumors, and the water cools itself in the glasses. Oh! Perlimplín... Where are you, Perlimplín?

(He exits on tiptoe. BELISA appears, dressed in a grand lacy nightgown. Her hair is loose, and her arms revealed, nude.)

BELISA: The servant perfumed this room with thyme and not with mint as I instructed... *(Goes toward the bed.)* And didn't even put on the bed the fine linens Marcolfa has...

(At this moment, soft guitar music is heard. BELISA crosses her hands over her breasts.)

BELISA: Oh! He who will look for me with ardor will find me. My thirst is never quenched, like the thirst is never quenched of the satyrs who eject water in the fountains.

(The music continues.)

BELISA: Oh! What music, my God. What music! Like the hot down of the swans... Oh! Is it I? Or is it the music? *(She throws upon her shoulders a great red velvet cape and strolls about the room. The music stops and five whistles are heard.)*

BELISA: There are five!

(PERLIMPLÍN appears.)

PERLIMPLÍN: Do I disturb?

BELISA: How is it possible?

PERLIMPLÍN: Are you sleepy?

BELISA: *(Ironically.)* Sleep?

PERLIMPLÍN: The night has become a bit cold.
(*He rubs his hands together. Pause.*)
BELISA: (*Firmly.*) Perlimplín.
PERLIMPLÍN: (*Trembling.*) What do you want?
BELISA: (*Vaguely.*) It's a pretty name. Perlimplín.
PERLIMPLÍN: Much prettier is yours. Belisa.
BELISA: (*Laughing.*) Oh! Thank you!
(*Short pause.*)
PERLIMPLÍN: I wanted to tell you something.
BELISA: And it is?
PERLIMPLÍN: I have delayed in making up my mind... But...
BELISA: Say it.
PERLIMPLÍN: Belisa... I love you!
BELISA: Oh, young gentleman... that is your obligation.
PERLIMPLÍN: Yes?
BELISA: Yes.
PERLIMPLÍN: But why yes?
BELISA: (*With mock endearment.*) Because it's yes.
PERLIMPLÍN: No.
BELISA: Perlimplín!
PERLIMPLÍN: No, Belisa. Before I married you, I didn't want you.
BELISA: (*Drolly.*) What do you say?
PERLIMPLÍN: I married... for what it would be, but I didn't want you. I couldn't have possibly imagined your body until I saw it through the keyhole when you were dressing as a bride. And it was then that I felt love. Then! Like a deep cut of a blade in my throat.
BELISA: (*Intrigued.*) But, and the other women?
PERLIMPLÍN: What women?
BELISA: The ones you knew before.
PERLIMPLÍN: But, are there other women?
BELISA: You astonish me.
PERLIMPLÍN: I'm the first to be astonished.
(*Pause. Five whistles are heard.*)
PERLIMPLÍN: What is that?
BELISA: The clock.
PERLIMPLÍN: Is it five?
BELISA: Time to sleep.
PERLIMPLÍN: Do I have your permission to take off my dress-coat?

BELISA: Of course, *(Yawning.)* hubby-wubby. And turn off the light, if you like.

(PERLIMPLÍN turns off the light.)

PERLIMPLÍN: *(Softly.)* Belisa.

BELISA: *(Loudly.)* What, my baby?

PERLIMPLÍN: *(Softly.)* I've turned off the light.

BELISA: *(Drolly.)* I see.

PERLIMPLÍN: *(Even softer.)* Belisa…

BELISA: *(Loudly.)* What, enchantment?

PERLIMPLÍN: I adore you.

(Two DUENDES, entering from opposite sides of the stage, draw a gray curtain. Theater in half-light. With a sweet, dream-like tone, flutes are heard. They should be two children. They sit on the prompter's box, facing the audience.)

DUENDE #1: And… how goes it with you through the nighty-night?

DUENDE #2: Neither good nor bad, my dear acolyte.

DUENDE #1: So here we are.

DUENDE #2: And what do you think? It's always fun to cover other people's flaws.

DUENDE #1: So that later the public can uncover them.

DUENDE #2: Because if precautions aren't taken to cover things…

DUENDE #1: They are never ever discovered.

DUENDE #2: And without this covering and uncovering…

DUENDE #1: What would become of the poor people?

DUENDE #2: *(Looking at curtain.)* Not a slit left.

DUENDE #1: Because today's slits will be dark tomorrow.

(They laugh.)

DUENDE #2: When things are clear…

DUENDE #1: Man thinks he has no need of discovering them…

DUENDE #2: And he goes to the dark to discover secrets he already knew.

DUENDE #1: But why else are we here? The duendes! Demons…

DUENDE #2: Of the night. You knew Perlimplín?

DUENDE #1: Since I was a child.

DUENDE #2: And Belisa?

DUENDE #1: As well. Her room gave off such an intense perfume that I fell asleep and woke up between her cat's claws.

(They laugh.)

DUENDE #2: This affair was…

DUENDE #1: Very transparent.

DUENDE #2: The whole world imagined it.

DUENDE #1: And the rumors fled toward more mysterious matters.

DUENDE #2: That's why our effective and highly personable mask must not be uncovered.

DUENDE #1: No, they mustn't find out.

DUENDE #2: Perlimplín's soul, small and scared like a newborn duckling, is enriched and exalted in these moments.

(They laugh.)

DUENDE #1: The public is impatient.

DUENDE #2: And rightly so. Let's go?

DUENDE #1: Let's go. I already feel a sweet chill on my back.

DUENDE #2: Five cool dawn camellias have opened in the bedroom walls.

DUENDE #1: Five balconies over the city.

(They rise and throw upon themselves great blue hoods.)

DUENDE #2: Don Perlimplín. Are we doing you a good or bad turn?

DUENDE #1: Good…because it's not fair to present to the public's eyes the misfortune of a good man.

DUENDE #2: It's true, dear little acolyte; because it's not the same to say "I have seen," than "They say."

DUENDE #1: Tomorrow everyone will know.

DUENDE #2: And that's what we desire.

DUENDE #1: Rumors throughout the world.

DUENDE #2: Tsk!

(Flutes begin.)

DUENDE #1: Shall we go through the nighty-night?

DUENDE #2: Let's go now, dear acolyte.

DUENDE #1: Now?

DUENDE #2: Now.

(They draw the curtain. DON PERLIMPLÍN appears in bed with enormous horns, golden and blossoming, on his head. BELISA is at his side. In the background, the five balconies are wide open. Through them, the white light of dawn shines.)

PERLIMPLÍN: *(Waking.)* Belisa, Belisa, answer!

BELISA: *(Pretending to wake.)* Perlimpli-pee-nee-wee, what do you want?

PERLIMPLÍN: Tell me now.

BELISA: What will I tell you? That I fell asleep much earlier than you.

(PERLIMPLÍN gets out of bed. He wears his dress-coat.)

PERLIMPLÍN: Why are the balconies open?

BELISA: Because tonight the wind has blown like never before.

PERLIMPLÍN: Why do the balconies have five ladders that go down to the ground?

BELISA: Because that's the custom in my mother's country.

PERLIMPLÍN: And whose are they, those five hats that I see below the balconies?

BELISA: *(Jumping out of bed.)* Of the little drunks that come and go, Perlimpli-nee-wee. Love!

(PERLIMPLÍN looks at her. He is lost in her.)

PERLIMPLÍN: Belisa! Belisa! And why not? You explain everything so well. I'm satisfied. Why shouldn't it be like this?

BELISA: *(With mock endearment.)* I do not tell lies.

PERLIMPLÍN: And every minute I want you more!

BELISA: That's why I like it.

PERLIMPLÍN: For the first time in my life I am happy.

(He draws near and embraces her. And just as quickly he breaks from her brusquely.)

PERLIMPLÍN: Belisa? Who has kissed you? Do not lie. I know it!

BELISA: *(Putting her hair up.)* I believe you do! What a witty little hubby I have! *(Softly.)* You! You have kissed me.

PERLIMPLÍN: Yes. I have kissed you… But… If someone else kissed you… if someone else kissed you… Do you love me?

BELISA: *(Extending a bare arm to embrace him.)* Yes, little Perlimplín.

PERLIMPLÍN: Then… I don't care. *(He embraces her.)* And you, Belisa…?

BELISA: *(Softly, endearing.)* Yes! Yes! Yes!

PERLIMPLÍN: It seems like a dream.

BELISA: *(Reacting.)* Look, Perlimplín, close the balconies, because before long others will wake.

PERLIMPLÍN: What for? Since we two have slept quite enough, we'll watch the sun rise… Don't you like it?

BELISA: Yes, but…

(She sits on the bed.)

PERLIMPLÍN: Never have I seen the sun rise…

(BELISA, surrendering to her exhaustion, throws herself upon the pillows.)

PERLIMPLÍN: It's a spectacle that… it can't be real… it moves me… Don't you like it? *(He goes toward the bed.)* Belisa? Are you sleeping?

BELISA: *(In midst of slumber.)* Yes.

(PERLIMPLÍN, on tiptoe, covers her with the red cape. An intense golden light comes through the balconies. Flock of black paper birds goes by midst the sound of morning bells. PERLIMPLÍN sits on the edge of the bed.)

PERLIMPLÍN: Love, love

That is wounded.
Wounded of love expended.
Wounded,
Dying of love.
Tell everyone that the nightingale lamented.
Scalpel of four edges.
Throat cut and wretched.
Take my hand, love.
For I come badly wounded.
Wounded!
Wounded of love expended.
Dying of love!
(CURTAIN.)

Maggie Stewart as Belisa and Andy Weems as Don Perlimplín
from *The Love of Don Perlimplín for Belisa in the Garden*
University of California—San Diego, 1988

photo from U.C.S.D. Theater archives

FRAME THREE

DON PERLIMPLÍN'S dining room. The perspectives are deliciously wrong. Painted objects on the table. A primitive dinner.

PERLIMPLÍN: Will you do as I say?

MARCOLFA: *(Crying.)* Forget it, lord.

PERLIMPLÍN: Marcolfa, why do you keep crying?

MARCOLFA: Because of what you know, your grace. On the wedding night, five people came in through the balconies. Five! Men from all over the world. And you, without knowing...

PERLIMPLÍN: It does not matter.

MARCOLFA: Imagine! Yesterday I saw her with another.

PERLIMPLÍN: *(Intrigued.)* How so?

MARCOLFA: And she didn't hide from me.

PERLIMPLÍN: But I am happy, Marcolfa.

MARCOLFA: My master astonishes me.

PERLIMPLÍN: Happy like you would not believe. I have learned so much. And above all, I can imagine things.

MARCOLFA: You love her too much.

PERLIMPLÍN: Not as much as she deserves.

MARCOLFA: Here she comes.

PERLIMPLÍN: Get out.

(MARCOLFA exits. PERLIMPLÍN hides in a corner. BELISA appears.)

BELISA: And I haven't even seen him. In my stroll through the grove, all followed me except him. He must be dark and his kisses must linger and burn like saffron and clove. Sometimes he walks below my balconies and waves his hand slowly in a greeting that makes my breasts tremble.

PERLIMPLÍN: Hmm!

BELISA: *(Turning.)* Oh! What a fright you've given me.

(PERLIMPLÍN draws closer to her.)

PERLIMPLÍN: *(Affectionately.)* I notice you talk to yourself.

BELISA: *(Annoyed.)* Get off me!

PERLIMPLÍN: Would you like to take a stroll?

BELISA: No.

PERLIMPLÍN: Would you like to go to the bakery?

BELISA: I said no.

PERLIMPLÍN: Sorry.

(A stone in which a letter is rolled falls through the balcony. PERLIMPLÍN picks it up.)

BELISA: Give me!

PERLIMPLÍN: Why?

BELISA: Because it's mine.

PERLIMPLÍN: *(Mocking.)* And who told you?

BELISA: Perlimplín! Don't read it!

PERLIMPLÍN: *(Forcefully, but still in jest.)* What do you mean?

BELISA: *(Crying.)* Give me that letter.

PERLIMPLÍN: *(Drawing near.)* Poor Belisa! Because I understand the state you are in, I will hand you this piece of paper that means so much to you...

(BELISA grabs the letter and slips it inside her dress between her breasts.)

PERLIMPLÍN: I notice things. And although they wound me deeply, I understand you live in a drama.

BELISA: *(Tenderly.)* Perlimplín!

PERLIMPLÍN: I know you are unfaithful and you will continue to be.

BELISA: *(Like a spoiled child.)* I've never known more of a man than my Perlimplínee-wee...

PERLIMPLÍN: That's why I want to help you as every good husband should when his wife is a model of virtue... Look.

(He closes the doors and takes on a mysterious air.)

PERLIMPLÍN: I know everything... I noticed immediately. You are young, and I am old... what can we do?... But I understand perfectly.

(Pause.)

PERLIMPLÍN: *(Softly.)* Has he come by here?

BELISA: Twice.

PERLIMPLÍN: And he's given you signs...?

BELISA: Yes... but in a rather contemptuous manner... and that hurts!

PERLIMPLÍN: Never fear. Fifteen days ago I saw this young man for the first time. I tell you in all sincerity: His beauty dazzled me. Never have I seen a man in whom the virile and the delicate combine in such a harmonious fashion. Without knowing why, I thought of you.

BELISA: I haven't seen his face... but...

PERLIMPLÍN: Do not be afraid to talk to me... I know you love him... Now, I love you as if I were your father... I am far from foolishness... so...

BELISA: He writes me letters.

PERLIMPLÍN: I know.

BELISA: But he won't show himself.

PERLIMPLÍN: Strange.

BELISA: And it seems… as if he scorns me…

PERLIMPLÍN: *(Intrigued.)* What?

BELISA: The letters of the other men I have received… and ones I did not answer, because I had my little hubby, spoke of faraway lands, dreams, and wounded loves… but his letters… look…

PERLIMPLÍN: He speaks without fear.

BELISA: He speaks of me… of my body….

PERLIMPLÍN: *(Caressing her.)* Of your body!

BELISA: "Why do I want your soul?" he says. "The soul is claimed by the weak, by crippled heroes and sickly folk. The beautiful souls are on death's border, stooped over, with white hair and withered hands. Belisa, it's not your soul I desire, but your white and delicate body trembling…"

PERLIMPLÍN: Who could this lovely young man be?

BELISA: No one knows.

PERLIMPLÍN: *(Inquisitive.)* No one?

BELISA: I've asked all my friends.

PERLIMPLÍN: *(Mysterious yet firm.)* And if I told you I knew him?

BELISA: Is it possible?

PERLIMPLÍN: Wait. *(He goes to the balcony.)* Here he is.

BELISA: *(Running.)* Yes?

PERLIMPLÍN: He just turned the corner.

BELISA: *(Out of breath.)* Oh!

PERLIMPLÍN: Since I am old, I want to sacrifice myself for you… What I will do, no one has ever done. But I am already gone from this world, and the ridiculous morals of the public. Good-bye.

BELISA: Where are you going?

PERLIMPLÍN: *(At the door, grandly.)* Much later you will know everything. Much later!

(CURTAIN.)

Maggie Stewart as Belisa
from *The Love of Don Perlimplín for Belisa in the Garden*
University of California—San Diego, 1988

photo from U.C.S.D. Theater archives

FRAME FOUR

*Garden of cypresses and oranges. As the curtain rises, PERLIMPLÍN and
MARCOLFA are by the hedge.*

MARCOLFA: Is it time yet?

PERLIMPLÍN: No. It is not time yet.

MARCOLFA: But, what did you think, my lord?

PERLIMPLÍN: Everything I had not thought of before.

MARCOLFA: *(Crying.)* It's my fault.

PERLIMPLÍN: Oh! If you could see what gratitude my heart holds for you.

MARCOLFA: Before, everything was clear. I would bring him his coffee
with milk and grapes in the morning...

PERLIMPLÍN: Yes... Grapes. Grapes? But...And me? I feel like a hundred
years have passed. Before, I could not think of the extraordinary things
the world has to offer...I would stay indoors...And now! Belisa's love
has given me this precious treasure that I ignored... See? I close my eyes
now and... I see what I want... for example... my mother when she was
visited by the Fairies of the vicinity... Oh! You know how the Fairies
are... teeny tiny... They are quite admirable... Why, they can dance on
my little finger.

MARCOLFA: Yes. Yes, the Fairies, the Fairies, but... and the other?

PERLIMPLÍN: The other...? Ah! *(With pleasure.)* What did you tell my
wife?

MARCOLFA: Although I am not very good at this sort of thing, I told her
what the master instructed... that this gentleman... would come to the
garden tonight at ten o'clock precisely, wrapped, as always, in his red
cape.

PERLIMPLÍN: And she...?

MARCOLFA: She glowed like a geranium in full bloom, put her hands over
her heart, and kissed her beautiful braids of hair passionately.

PERLIMPLÍN: *(Enthused.)* Like a geranium? And...what did she say?

MARCOLFA: Sighed. Nothing else. But, what a sigh!

PERLIMPLÍN: Oh, yes!... Like no woman ever before! True?

MARCOLFA: Her love exceeds lunacy.

PERLIMPLÍN: *(Vibrantly.)* Just so! I need her to love that gentleman more
than her own body. And there's no doubt she loves him.

MARCOLFA: *(Crying.)* It scares me to hear him... But how is it possible?

Don Perlimplín, how is it possible? That you yourself stir in your wife
the worst of sins!

PERLIMPLÍN: Because Don Perlimplín has no honor. Because he only
wants to enjoy himself. You see! Tonight the new and unknown lover of
my mistress Belisa will come. What should I do but sing? *(Sings.)* Don
Perlimplín has no honor! Has no honor!

MARCOLFA: My lord, you should know that as of this moment, I am no
longer in your service. Servants have shame.

PERLIMPLÍN: Oh, innocent Marcolfa! Tomorrow you will be free as a
bird… Stay until tomorrow… Now, go and do your duty. Will you do
as I say?

(MARCOLFA, walks away, drying her tears.)

MARCOLFA: What choice do I have? What choice?

PERLIMPLÍN: Good. That is how I like it.

*(A sweet serenade begins to play. DON PERLIMPLÍN hides behind a rose-
bush.)*

BELISA: *(From off, singing.)*
By the banks of the river
the night is wading.

VOICES: The night is wading.

BELISA: And on the breasts of Belisa
The branches die of love.

VOICES: The branches die of love.

PERLIMPLÍN: The branches die of love.

BELISA: The night sings naked
Over the bridges of March.

VOICES: Over the bridges of March.

BELISA: Belisa bathes her body
With salt water and valerian.

PERLIMPLÍN: The branches die of love.

BELISA: The night of anise and silver
Gleams on the rooftops.

VOICES: Gleams on the rooftops.

BELISA: Silver streams and mirrors
And the anise of your thighs so white.

PERLIMPLÍN: *(Weeping.)* The branches die of love.

*(BELISA appears in the garden. She is splendidly undressed. The moon
shines on her, revealing one gold breast, and the other of silver. A star shoots
by like a large cigar.)*

BELISA: What voices fill the air with sweet harmony this fragment of the night? I have felt your heart and your delicious weight on me, young gentleman of my soul… Oh!…yes!… The branches rustle…

(A man wrapped in a large bullfighter's cape appears, and crosses the garden cautiously.)

BELISA: He's here… Look at me…

(The man, with a wave of his hand, indicates that he will return.)

BELISA: Oh! Yes! Come back, my love! You, rootless and floating jasmine. The sky falls upon my back moist with sweat… Night! My night of mint and ultra-marine…

(BELISA'S sensual voice sounds like a rich gush of water in midst of the cool, peaceful night. PERLIMPLÍN appears.)

PERLIMPLÍN: *(Feigning surprise.)* What are you doing here?

BELISA: Strolling.

PERLIMPLÍN: And nothing else?

(Pause.)

BELISA: In the clear night.

PERLIMPLÍN: *(Spiritedly.)* What were you doing here?

BELISA: *(Surprised.)* But you didn't know?

PERLIMPLÍN: I do not know anything.

BELISA: *(Surpirsed.)* But you sent me the message.

PERLIMPLÍN: *(Lustfully.)* Belisa… you still wait for him?

BELISA: With more ardor than ever.

PERLIMPLÍN: *(Strongly.)* Why?

BELISA: Because I love him.

PERLIMPLÍN: *(Gently.)* Then he'll come.

BELISA: The smell of his flesh seeps through his clothes. I want him! Perlimplín, I love him! It is as though I am another woman.

PERLIMPLÍN: That is my triumph.

BELISA: What triumph?

PERLIMPLÍN: The triumph of my imagination.

BELISA: *(Tenderly.)* It is true you helped me love him.

PERLIMPLÍN: As now I will help you cry for him.

BELISA: *(Perplexed.)* Perlimplín, what are you saying?

(The clock strikes ten. Nightingales sing.)

PERLIMPLÍN: Now is the time.

BELISA: He will be here soon.

PERLIMPLÍN: He leaps the walls of my graden.

BELISA: Wrapped in his red cape.

PERLIMPLÍN: *(Drawing a dagger.)* Red like his blood.

BELISA: *(Restraining him.)* What are you going to do?

PERLIMPLÍN: *(Embracing her.)* Belisa, do you love him?

BELISA: *(Forcefully.)* Yes!

PERLIMPLÍN: Well, given that you love him so much, I don't want him to abandon you. Thus, so that he can be yours completely, it has occurred to me that the best I can do is to stick this dagger into his gallant heart. Would you like that?

BELISA: By God, Perlimplín!

PERLIMPLÍN: Doesn't it seem that way, my child? If he is dead, you can caress him always in your bed, so pale and pretty he'll be, without the fear that I'll stop loving you. He will love you with the infinite love of all souls, and I will be free of the clear nightmare of your body...magnificent! *(Embracing her.)* Your body!... that I could never unravel! *(Looking at the garden.)* Look from whence he comes... well and fine! Dear God, how beautiful, how beautiful he is... But let go, Belisa... Let go! *(He exits, running.)*

BELISA: *(Desperately.)* Marcolfa! Marcolfa, bring me the sword from the dining room, because I am going to run my husband's throat through! *(Shouting.)*

Don Perlimplín,

Husband so mean!

If you kill him,

I'll kill you clean.

Don Perlimplín!

Don Perlimplín!

(A man wrapped in a large red cape appears among the branches. He is wounded and unstable.)

BELISA: *(Embracing him.)* Who opened your veins, love, so that you fill my garden with blood! Let me see your face, if only for an instant. Oh! Who gave you death?... Who?

PERLIMPLÍN: *(Uncovering himself.)* Your husband has just killed me with this emerald dagger.

(He shows dagger stuck in his chest.)

BELISA: *(Frightened.)* Perlimplín!

PERLIMPLÍN: He ran through the fields, and you will not see him ever again. He killed me because he knew that I loved you like no one else... While he wounded me, he shouted "Belisa now has a soul!" Come closer. *(He rests on a bench.)*

BELISA: But what is this? You are wounded for real.

PERLIMPLÍN: Perlimplín killed me... Ah, Don Perlimplín! Old virgin without strength. You couldn't enjoy Belisa's body... Belisa's body was made for younger muscles and ardent lips... I, in turn, loved only your body... Your body! But he has killed me... with this burning branch of precious jewels.

BELISA: What have you done?

PERLIMPLÍN: *(Near death.)* Understand? I am my soul, and you are your body... Let me in this last moment, given that you have loved me so much, let me die in your embrace.

(BELISA draws closer, embraces him.)

BELISA: Yes... but, and the young man? Why did you lie to me?

PERLIMPLÍN: Young man!

(He closes his eyes. The scene is left in natural light. Marcolfa enters.)

MARCOLFA: Madam!

BELISA: *(Crying.)* Don Perlimplín has died.

MARCOLFA: I knew it! Now let us shroud the corpse with the young man's red cape, the very same cape with which he strolled below his very own balconies.

BELISA: *(Crying.)* I never believed it could be this complicated.

MARCOLFA: He realized much too late. I will make him a crown of flowers like the midday sun.

(BELISA is as if in another world now.)

BELISA: Perlimplín, what have you done?

MARCOLFA: Belisa, you are already another woman. You are dressed in the most glorious blood of my lord.

BELISA: But who was that man? Who was he?

MARCOLFA: The beautiful adolescent whose face you will never see.

BELISA: Yes. Yes, Marcolfa, I love him. I love him with all the strength in my flesh and soul. But where is the young man with the red cape? Dear God, where is he?

MARCOLFA: Don Perlimplín, sleep in peace... Do you hear her? Don Perlimplín... do you hear her?

(Bells ring.)

END OF PLAY

THE BLUE HORSE

By Erik Ehn

Lorca writes what is precisely so. The fearlessness of his precision is the strength of his abandon, like a kind of dancer (flamenco)—he makes decisive steps, without deliberation. Decision approaches the speed of thingness: Action is as precise as object, and object is too singular (of the moment) to be traded. You cannot read your way into a reading of Lorca or plan your way into a staging (you do not choose to be a genius or gay). You stage, you read as a full expression of who you are at a point in your life. Lorca is underproduced because the theater would rather talk about itself than be itself. Where other writers *influence*, Lorca (Faulkner, Rilke) possesses—he is malicious and unforgettable. Some poems in the world are arrows of love; Lorca is his poems, and he is the instant of the arrow's piercing.

His plays can be difficult to realize. Writers in Lorca's sway may have trouble finding actors who will "just say the words" (Lorcan drama is the drama of language first, situation and character second; picture is included as a form of address). "Just… just say—" is an inchoate appeal to an actor's sophisticated and mysterious access to grace—to an empty presence simultaneous with the sublime. Writers and actors are confused by a habit of training that invites an exploration of subtext. We are coached to treat text as the medium that misdirects meaning and experience for the sake of sophistication, that alchemizes emotion to the sublimely academic, that delays knowledge or interpretation for the sake of suspense (plot). Meaning (per this habit) is psychological: Hook a loudspeaker to the soul and hear her speak prose at a whisper. Text here is a game, subtext is words.

There are no words in Lorca. There is only text, and no subtext. His language slows action to anguished immobility—a Sebastian martyrdom (compare recent experiments in physics, where light is slowed to a crawl). Prose words signify. Words tormented by Lorca bleed significance. Habits of training need to change. We need to leave this protracted age of experiment (prose science) that values incremental correctness en route to comprehensibility. Go nowhere. Stand initially where the satisfaction of all potential is iconic in the anguish of a saint. Saint Text-Sebastian gathers life and death, celibacy and sex, heroic defeat and ridiculously costumed triumph at the moment of the martyr's pillar. Forgo methods. Just play.

> There's no enlightenment, no new age
> Only a blue horse and the dawn.

As with Zen, as with Euripides, as with moody and brilliant children, Lorca steps from center to center of paradox after paradox. His chief field is love. Love in Lorca is always wedded to the unlovely act. Principle comes to practice, the a priori state trembles into time. This must be, a rule of the universe. Lorca believes in God. God is love. Love is a law requiring the passionate union of maker with unmaking. In Lorca:

> The child loves age (loves and is defeated by; loves defeat)
> Romance loves compunction (loves and…)
> Effort loves the effortlessness it will never achieve

Most tragically of all, romance is most fatal: The poet is in love with the stage (the stage is the poet's opposite, the stage is where poetry is killed for its belief). Lorca is a Blake with a better sense of practical dramaturgy, alive in an age where the Marriage of Heaven and Hell is made more flagrantly problematic under fascism.

Lorca writes what is precisely so, then, like the advanced physicist, knows that location is a deep thing: spooky. Precision is a quality of experience, a condition of enlightenment. Precision is not one point, but a field, or the way of navigating a field. The precision of the dance is not in this step or this step; it is in the way, the spirit (duende) of the dance. A dancer with duende can make a precise dance with imprecise steps. A singer with duende sings more than the notes. The playwright (the poet martyred on the stage) is exactly paradoxical. Deep song. His exact(ing) images are themselves and the space around themselves, space made deep (terrible, incorrect, ridiculous, sacramental) through awareness of vulnerability and peril: Word is crucified on wordlessness.

Conventional theater (in process and presentation) suspends, anticipates, promises, then reflects. Lorca offers a theater of incarnation. Lorca breaks promises to a thousand pieces—promises are impossible in his land of perfect manifestation. He offers the childlike and doomed instant of love. We do not understand Lorca, and we cannot rehearse him. We love him, fail with him, in the sacrament of play.

POET IN NEW YORK

Poeta en Nueva York

by Federico García Lorca
selected poems in a new translation by Caridad Svich

1910

(intermezzo)

My eyes of nineteen hundred and ten
did not see the dead being buried,
nor the ashen fire that rose from the one who wept at dawn,
nor the heart that trembled like a cornered sea horse.

My eyes of nineteen hundred and ten
saw the white wall where the little girls pissed,
the bull's muzzle, the poisonous mushroom,
and an incomprehensible moon that illuminated
the dried lemon rinds under the hard black asses
of the bottles in the corners.

My eyes on the pony's neck,
on the pierced breast of Saint Rose as she slept,
on the rooftops of love, with moans and cool hands,
in the garden where cats feed on toads.

Attic where the ancient dust assembles statues and moss.
Boxes that keep the silence of devoured crabs.
In the place where dream collides with reality.
My small eyes are there.

Don't ask me anything. I've seen how things
that seek their own way find the void instead.
There is a hollow pain in the uninhabited air
And completely dressed creatures in my eyes—no one naked there.

—New York, August 1929

Fable and Roundelay
of Three Friends

Enrique,
Emilio,
Lorenzo.
The three of them were frozen:
Enrique in the world of beds,
Emilio in the world of eyes and wounded hands,
Lorenzo in the world of roofless universities.

Lorenzo,
Emilio,
Enrique.
The three of them were burned:
Lorenzo in the world of leaves and billiard balls,
Emilio in the world of blood and white needles,
Enrique in the world of the dead and abandoned newspapers.

Lorenzo,
Emilio,
Enrique.
The three of them were buried:
Lorenzo in Flora's breast,
Emilio in the shot of stiff gin forgotten in the glass,
Enrique in the ant, the sea, the empty eyes of birds.

Lorenzo,
Emilio,
Enrique.
In my hands the three of them were:
three Chinese mountains,
three shadows of horses,
three fields of snow and a shelter of lilies
near the pigeon coops where the moon lies flat beneath the rooster.

One
and one
and one.
The three of them were mummified
with winter flies
with inkpots that the dogs piss and thistle-down spurns,
with the breeze that chills every mother's heart,
by Jupiter's white debris, where the drunks lunch on death.

Three
and two
and one.
I saw them lose themselves, crying and singing,
in a hen's egg,
in the night that exposed its skeleton of tobacco,
in my suffering, full of faces and the moon's piercing shrapnel,
in my delight of serrated wheels and whips,
in my chest unsettled with doves,
in my empty death graced by a lone mistaken passerby.

I had killed the fifth moon
and the fans and applause drank water from the fountains.
Lukewarm milk inside the new mothers
stirred the roses with a long white sorrow.

Enrique,
Emilio,
Lorenzo.
Diana is hard
but at times her breasts are clouded.
The white stone can throb in the blood of a deer
and the deer can dream through the eyes of a horse.

Where the pure shapes sank
under the chirping of daisies,
I knew they had murdered me.
They combed the cafés, cemeteries and churches for me,
pried open casks and cabinets,
destroyed three skeletons in order to pull out their gold teeth.

They couldn't find me anymore
They couldn't find me?
No. They couldn't find me.
But it was known that the sixth moon fled against the torrent,
and the sea—suddenly!—remembered
the names of all its drowned.

Dance of Death

The mask. Look how the mask
comes from Africa to New York.

The pepper trees are gone,
the tiny buds of phosphorus.
The camels with their torn flesh,
and the valleys of light the swan lifted with its beak
are also gone.

It was a barren time:
of the spike in the eye and the laminated cat
of tremendous bridges of rusted iron
and the deathly silence of cork.

It was the great reunion of dead animals
pierced by the swords of light;
the eternal joy of the hippopotamus with its hooves of ash
and of the gazelle with the house-leek in its throat.

In the withered, aimless solitude
The dented mask was dancing.
Half of the world was sand,
the other, mercury and dormant sunlight.

The mask. Look at the mask!
Sand, crocodile, and fear above New York.

Canyons of lime imprisoned the empty sky,
where the voices of those who die under the palm trees were heard,
A pure, stripped sky, identical with itself,
with the down and sharp-edged iris of its invisible mountains,

did away with the slender stems of song
and was swept away in the deluge filled with sap,
through the stillness of the last profiles,
picking up shards of mirror with its tail.

When the Chinaman wept on the roof
upon not finding the naked body of his wife,
and the bank director examined the manometer
that measures money's cruel silence,
the mask approached Wall Street.

It is not a strange place for the dance
This cemetery niche that turns eyes yellow.
Between the sphinx and the bank vault, there is a taut thread
that pierces the heart of all poor children.
The primitive impulse dances with the mechanical impulse,
unaware in its frenzy of the original light.
Because if the wheel forgets its formula,
it will sing naked with herds of horses;
and if a flame burns the frozen blueprints,
the sky will have to flee before the tumult of windows.

This isn't a strange place for the dance. I say it.
The mask will dance among columns of blood and numbers,
among hurricanes of gold and the wails of the unemployed,
who will howl, in the coal-blasted night, for your dark time.
Oh savage, impudent North America! Oh savage!
Stretched out on the snow's frontier.

The mask. Look at the mask!
What a wave of mire and fireflies over New York!

I was on the terrace wrestling with the moon.
Swarms of windows riddled one of the night's thighs.
The sweet cows of the skies drunk from my eyes
and the long-oared breezes
struck the ashen windows on Broadway.

The drop of blood looked for light in the star's yolk
so as to seem a dead apple seed.
The prairie made barren by the shepherds,
trembled in fear like a mollusk without its shell.

But it is not the dead who dance,
of this I'm certain.
The dead are drunk, devouring their own hands.
It is the others who dance with the mask and the guitar,
it is the others, drunk on silver, the cold men
who sleep where thighs and hard flames come to rest,
who seek the earthworm in a landscape of fire escapes,
who drink a dead girl's tears at the bank
or eat pyramids of dawn on the tiny street corners.

Don't let the Pope dance!
No, don't let the Pope dance!
Nor the king
nor the millionaire with blue teeth
nor the barren dancers of the cathedrals,
nor builders, nor emeralds, nor the mad,
nor the sodomites.
Only the mask.
This mask of ancient scarlet fever.
Only this mask!

Cobras will hiss on the top floors
Nettles will shake courtyards and terraces,
The Stock Exchange will be a pyramid of moss.
Jungle vines will rise behind the rifles
and very soon, very soon, very soon
Oh, Wall Street!

The mask. Look at the mask.
How it spews its forest poison
Throughout the imperfect anguish of New York!

—December 1929

Landscape of the Vomiting Crowd

(Dusk in Coney Island)

The fat lady came first
tearing out roots and moistening drumskins.
The fat lady
who turns dying octopuses inside out.
The fat lady, the moon's enemy,
ran through the streets and abandoned buildings
leaving the tiny skulls of pigeons in the corners
awakening the furies of last centuries' feasts
calling up the bread demon through the sky's barren hills
and filtering a longing for light into the subterranean tunnels.
They're the graveyards. I know. They're the graveyards
and the sorrow of kitchens buried in the sand.
They're the dead, the pheasants and apples of another time
that push themselves down our throats.

There were rumblings from the jungle of vomit
with the empty women, with hot wax children
with fermented trees and tireless waiters
who serve plates of salt beneath the harps of saliva.
There's no cure, my child, vomit! There's no cure.
It's the vomit of hussars over the breasts of their whores,
nor the vomit of a cat who accidentally swallowed a toad.
It's the dead who scratch with their hands of dirt
on the flint gates where clouds and desserts rot.

The fat lady came first
with the crowds from the ships, taverns and gardens.
The vomit delicately shook its drums
among some little girls of blood
who begged for the moon's protection.
Woe is I! Woe is I! Woe is I!

This look on my face was mine, but now it is no longer,
this look that trembles nakedly for liquor
and launches incredible ships
through the anemones of the docks.
I protect myself with this look
that flows through the waves where dawn doesn't dare.
I, armless poet, lost
in the vomiting crowd,
without a warm horse to cut
the thick moss from my temples.

But the fat lady went on
and the crowd kept looking for the drugstores
where the bitter tropic sets.
Only when the flag was raised and the first dogs arrived
did the entire city rush to the railings of the boardwalk.

—New York, December 29, 1929

Landscape of the Pissing Crowd

(Battery Park Nocturne)

The men were by themselves
as the last of the bicycles sped by.
The women were by themselves
waiting for the death of the boy in the Japanese sailboat.
They stayed by themselves,
dreaming of the open beaks of dying birds,
the sharp parasol that punctures
a recently squashed frog,
beneath a silence of a thousand ears
and tiny mouths of water
in the canyons that resist
the violent attack of the moon.
The boy on the sailboat was crying, and hearts were breaking
anguished at bearing witness to and keeping vigil over all things
and because there still could be heard
on the sky-blue ground riddled with black footprints
the crying of obscure names, saliva, and chrome radios.
It doesn't matter if the boy is silenced when stuck with the last pin,
nor if the breeze is defeated in the flowering of cotton,
because there is a world of death whose perpetual sailors
will appear in the arches and will freeze you from behind the trees.
It's useless to look for the bend
where night loses its way
and waits in ambush for a silence that doesn't have
torn clothes, shells, and weeping,
because even the tiny feast of a spider
is enough to break the equilibrium of a whole sky.
There's no remedy for the cries from the Japanese sailboat
nor for those shadowy folk who stumble on the city's curbs.
The countryside bites its own tail in order to gather all roots into one

and a ball of yarn looks anxiously in the grass for its unrealized
longitude.
The Moon! The police. The foghorns of the ocean-liners!
Facades of urine, of smoke, anemones, rubbers.
Everything is broken by the night,
with its legs spread on the terraces.
everything is broken by the tepid faucets
of a terribly silent fountain.
Oh crowds! Oh whores! Oh soldiers!
We will have to travel through the eyes of idiots, open country where
tame, coiled cobras hiss,
landscapes full of graves that yield the ripest apples,
so that the unmitigated light
that the rich dread from behind their magnifying glasses, will come,
the odor of a single corpse reeking of rats and lilies,
so that those that can piss next to the sound of someone whimpering
may burn
or we can come to know, through the glass, that no wave is like any
other.

Murder

(Two Voices at Dawn on Riverside Drive)

—How did it happen?
—A gash on the cheek.
That's all!
A fingernail that pinches the stem
A pin that drives
Until it finds a scream's smallest roots
And the sea stops moving.
—How, how did it happen?
—Like this.
—Leave be! Like that?
—Yes.
The heart came out all by itself.
—Oh, have pity on me!

Cow

The wounded cow lay down
Trees and streams climbed over its horns
Its muzzle bled in the sky.

Its muzzle of bees
Under the lingering mustache of drool
A white cry brought the morning to its feet.

The dead cows and the live ones
flush of light or honey from the stable
bellowed with half-closed eyes.

Let the roots
and that boy who is sharpening his razor
know
that they may now eat the cow.

Above them, light
and jugulars turn pale.
Four hoofs tremble in the air.

Let the moon
and the night of yellow rocks
know
that the ashen cow has gone.

That is has gone bellowing
through the debris of the still skies
where the drunks lunch on death.

Death

What effort!
What an effort for a horse to be a dog!
What effort for a dog to be a swallow!
What effort for a swallow to be a bee!
What effort for a bee to be a horse!
And the horse,
what a sharp arrow it squeezes from the rose
what a gray rose rises from its lips!
And the rose,
what a rain of lights and cries
Does it tie in the living sugar of its trunk.
And the sugar,
what tiny daggers does it dream in its vigil!
And the tiny daggers,
what a moon without stables, what nakedness,
what eternal, blushing skin, they seek!
And I, through the eaves,
what burning angel do I seek, and am I!
But the arc of gypsum
how great, how invisible, how small
and without effort.

Nocturne of Emptiness

I.

To see if everything has gone
to see the empty spaces and the dresses,
give me your lunar glove
your other glove of grass,
my love!

The air can tear dead snails
from the elephant's lung
and blow the frostbit worms
from the yolks of light or apples.

Impassive faces sail
beneath the faint uproar of the grass
and in the corner is the toad's tiny chest
with a troubled heart, and mandolin.

On the great deserted square,
the cow's freshly severed head bellows
and the shapes that sought the serpent's path
were turned into hard cut glass.

To see if everything has gone
give me your hollow silence, my love,
School-day nostalgia and mournful sky.
To see if everything has gone!

Inside you, my love, what a silence
of wrecked trains runs through your flesh!
How many mummies' arms in bloom!
What sky without end, love, what a sky!

Stone in water, voice on the breeze
love's limits flee their bleeding trunk.
You have only to touch the pulse of our current love
and flowers sprout over the other children.

To see if everything has gone
To see the empty spaces where clouds and rivers used to be
Give me your laurel branches, love,
To see if everything has gone.

A pure emptiness circles the dawn through you, through me
preserving the traces of the branches of blood
and an outline of tranquil gypsum that records
the punctured moon's instant sorrow.

Look at the concrete shapes in search of their void
Stray dogs and half-eaten apples
Look at the anxiety, the anguish of this sad fossilized world
that can't find the rhythm of its first sob.

When I search the bed for murmuring thread,
you come, my love, to cover my roof.
The hollow of an anthill can fill the air
but you keep moaning without direction through my eyes.

No, not through my eyes, for you show me
four rivers wrapped tightly around your arm.
In the hard cell where the imprisoned moon
devours a sailor in front of the children.

To see if everything has gone
constant love, fleeting love! No, do not give me your emptiness
for mine is already traveling through the air!
Pity on me, on you, on the breeze!
To see if everything has gone.

II.

I.
With the white, white hollow of a horse,
Manes of ash. Plaza, pure and bent.

I.
Hollow pierced, armpits ruptured.
Like a neutered grape's dry skin and asbestos at dawn.

All the light in the world fits in one eye.
The rooster crows and his song lasts longer than his wings.

I.
With the white, white hollow of a horse
Surrounded by spectators with ants on their tongues.

In the cold's circus with its unmutilated profile
Among the ruined columns of bloodless cheeks.

I.
My emptiness without you, city, without your voracious dead
Rider through my life finally at anchor.

I.

There's no enlightenment, no new age.
Only a blue horse and the dawn.

Landscape with Two Graves and an Assyrian Dog

Friend,
Get up so you can hear
the Assyrian dog howl.
Cancer's three nymphs have been dancing,
my son.
They brought mountains of red sealing wax
and stiff linens to the place where cancer slept.

The horse has an eye in its neck
and the moon was in a sky so cold
that she had to tear open her mound of Venus
and drown the ancient cemeteries in blood and ash.

Friend,
wake up, for the mountains do not breathe yet
and the grass of my heart is somewhere else.
It does not matter if you are full of sea-water.
I loved a child once for a long time
who had a nib on his tongue
and we lived for a hundred years inside a knife.
Wake up. Be quiet. Listen. Sit up.
The howling
is a long purple tongue that releases
terrifying ants, and the liquor of lilies.
It draws near the rock now. Do not spread out your roots!
It is closer now. Wail. Do not sob in your dreams, friend.

Friend!
Get up so you can hear
The Assyrian dog howl.

Cry to Rome

(From the Tower of the Chrysler Building)

Apples lightly wounded
by slender, silver rapiers,
clouds torn apart by a coral hand
that carries on its back an almond of fire,
arsenic fish like sharks,
sharks like teardrops that blind the masses,
roses that wound
and needles that live in blood's narrow streams,
enemy worlds and worm-covered loves
will fall on you. Will fall on the great dome
that anoints the military tongues with oil,
where a man pisses on a resplendent dove
and spits crushed coal
surrounded by thousands of small bells.

Because there is no one to hand out the bread and wine
No one to make the grass grow in the mouths of the dead
No one to unfold the linens of slumber
No one to weep for the wounded elephants.
There are only a million blacksmiths
forging chains for tomorrow's children.
There are only a million carpenters
making coffins that do not bear a cross.
There is only a crowd of lamentations
unbuttoning their clothes in anticipation of the bullets.
The man who spurns the dove should speak
should scream naked between the columns,
and should inject himself with leprosy
and cry such a horrible cry
that his rings and diamond telephones will dissolve.
But the man dressed in white
ignores the spike's mystery
ignores the moans of the women giving birth

ignores the fact that Christ can still give water
ignores the fact that the coin burns the prodigy's kiss
and offers the blood of the lamb to the pheasant's stupid beak.

The schoolteachers show the children
a wondrous light that comes from the mountains;
but what arrives is a junction of sewers
where cholera's shadowy nymphs scream.

The teachers point devoutly to the enormous incense-filled domes
but beneath the statues there is no love.
There is no love behind the eyes' fixed glass stare
Love is in the flesh torn by thirst
in the tiny huts that struggle against the flood
Love is in the ditch where the serpents of hunger writhe;
in the sad sea that rocks the skeletons of seagulls
and in the dark tormenting kiss beneath the pillows.
But the old man with translucent hands
will say: Love, love, love
proclaimed by millions of the dying;
will say: Love, love, love
midst affection's trembling flame;
will say: Peace, peace, peace
among the shivering knives and long hairs of dynamite;
he will say: Love, love, love
until his lips turn silver.

In the mean time, in the mean time, oh! In the mean time,
the blacks who remove the spittoons
the boys who tremble beneath the pallid terror of the executives,
the women who drown in mineral oil,
the multitude with their hammers, violins or clouds—
You must shout in front of the domes,
You must shout crazy with fire
You must shout crazy with snow
You must shout with your head full of excrement,
You must shout as if all the nights had come together,
You must shout with a voice so broken
that the cities tremble like little girls

and knock down the prisons of oil and music.
Because we want our daily bread,
older in bloom and perennially harvested tenderness
because we want Earth's will to be done,
for it gives its bounty to all of us.

Ode to Walt Whitman

By the East River and the Bronx
the young men were singing, exposing their waists,
with the wheel, with oil, leather and the hammer
Ninety thousand miners taking silver from the rocks
and children drawing stairs and perspectives.

But none of them slept
none of them wanted to be the river
none of them loved the huge leaves
none of them loved the shoreline's blue tongue.

By the East River and Queensboro
the young men wrestled with industry
and the Jews sold circumcision's rose
to the river faun
and the sky let loose over the bridges and rooftops
herds of bison driven by the wind.

But none of them stopped
none of them wanted to be a cloud
none of them looked for ferns
or the tambourine's yellow wheel.

When the moon rises
the pulleys will spin to unsettle the sky;
a border of needles will fence in memory
and the hearses will carry away the unemployed.

New York of mire
New York of wire and death
What angel do you keep hidden in your cheek?
What perfect voice will speak the truth of wheat?
Who, the terrible dream of your bruised anemones?

Not for a single moment, old beautiful Walt Whitman,
have I failed to see your beard full of butterflies
nor your corduroy shoulders frayed by the moon,
nor your virginal Apollonian thighs
nor your voice like a column of ash;
old man, beautiful as the mist
you cried like a bird
with its sex pierced by a needle,
satyr's enemy, vine's enemy,
and lover of bodies under the rough cloth.

Nor for a single moment, virile beauty
who among mountains of coal, billboards and railways
dreamed of being a river and sleeping like a river
with that mate who would place in your breast
the small ache of an ignorant leopard.

Not for a single moment, Adam of blood, macho,
man alone at sea, old beautiful Walt Whitman,
because on penthouse roofs
gathered at bars
emerging in bunches from the sewers
trembling between the legs of chauffeurs
or whirling on absinthe-soaked floors
the queers, Walt Whitman, the queers, point you out

He's one, too! He's one, too! And they throw themselves
on your luminous, chaste beard,
blondes from the north, blacks from the sands
crowds of wails and gestures,
like cats and serpents,
the queers, Walt Whitman, the queers
full of tears, flesh for the whip,
boot or bite of lion-tamers.

He's one, too! He's one, too! Stained fingers
point to the edge of your dream
when a friend eats your apple
with its faint taste of gasoline
and the sun sings in the navels
of the young men who play under the bridges.

But you weren't looking for the scratched eyes
nor the darkest swamp where children are submerged
nor the frozen saliva
nor the curves, wounded like a frog's belly,
that the queers wear in cars and on terraces
while the moon lashes them on terror's corners.

You looked for a naked body that would be like a river
Bull and dream who would join the wheel with seaweed
father of your agony, camellia of your death
who would moan in the blaze of your hidden equator.

Because it's right that a man should not look for his delight
in tomorrow morning's jungle of blood.
The sky has shores where life can be avoided
and there are bodies that shouldn't repeat themselves in the dawn.

Agony, agony, dream, ferment and dream
This is the world, my friend, agony, agony
The dead decompose beneath the city clocks
war passes by crying with a million gray rats
the rich give their mistresses
small brilliant dying objects
and life is neither noble, nor good, nor sacred.

Man can, if he wants, channel his desire
through a coral vein or a heavenly nude
Tomorrow's loves will be rocks and Time
a breeze that drifts drowsily through the branches.

That is why I do not raise my voice, old Walt Whitman
against the boy who writes
a girl's name on his pillow
nor against the young man who dresses as a bride
in the darkness of the closet,
nor against the lonely souls in casinos
who drink prostitute's water with disgust,
nor against the men with that dirty look in their eyes
who love men and burn their lips in silence.

But yes, against you, urban queers
of swollen flesh and unclean thoughts.
Mothers of mud. Harpies. Sleepless enemies
of Love that bestows crowns of joy.

Against you always, who give young men
foul death with drops of bitter poison.
Against you always,
Fairies of North America
Pájaros of Havana
Jotos of Mexico
Sarasas of Cadiz
Apios of Seville
Cancos of Madrid
Floras of Alicante,
Adelaidas of Portugal.

Queers of the world, murderers of doves!
Slaves of women. Boudoir bitches.
On display in the public square like feverish fans
or ambushed in the rigid landscapes of hemlock.

There is no mercy! Death
flows from your eyes
and gathers gray flowers at the mire's edge.
There is no mercy! Attention!
That the confused, the pure,
the classical, the famous, the beggars
close the doors of the bacchanal to you.

And you, beautiful Walt Whitman, asleep
on the banks of the Hudson
with your beard facing the Pole and your hands open
Soft clay or snow, your tongue calls for
mates to keep watch over your bodiless gazelle.
Sleep on, nothing remains
A dance of walls stirs the prairies
and America drowns itself in machines and tears.
I want the powerful air from the deepest night
to blow away the flowers and inscriptions
from the arch where you sleep
and a black child to let the rich whites know
that the spike's reign is coming.

The *Son* of the Blacks in Cuba

When the full moon comes
I will go to Santiago in Cuba.
I will go to Santiago.
In a car of black water.
I will go to Santiago.
The thatch huts will sing
I will go to Santiago.
When the palm wants to be a stork
I will go to Santiago.
And when the plantain wants to be a sea wasp
I will go to Santiago.
With Fonseca's blond head
I will go to Santiago.
And with Romeo and Juliet's rose
I will go to Santiago.
A paper ocean and silver coins
I will go to Santiago.
Oh Cuba, oh rhythm of dried seeds!
I will go to Santiago.
Oh fiery waist and drop of wood!
I will go to Santiago.
Harp of living tree trunks. Crocodile. Tobacco blossom.
I will go to Santiago.
I always said I would go to Santiago
in a car of black water.
I will go to Santiago.
Wind and liquor on wheels,
I will go to Santiago.
My coral in the darkness,
I will go to Santiago.
The ocean drowned in the sand,
I will go to Santiago.
White heat, rotting fruit.
I will go to Santiago.
Oh bovine coolness of the cane fields!
Oh Cuba! Oh curve of sigh and clay!
I will go to Santiago.

Mercedes Herrero as Mannequin
from *As Five Years Pass*
Intar Theatre, New York, New York, 1998

photo by Sturgis Warner

Some Thoughts on Lorca's *As Five Years Pass* and the Poetics of Poetic Theater

By Colin Teevan

> Spring...
> Too long...
> Gongula...
>
> > *Papyrus*, Ezra Pound.[1]

It would be overly simplistic to say that Lorca started his writing career as a poet with a keen sense of the dramatic and finished it, or at least had it terminated, at a point where he had evolved into a playwright capable of creating a three-dimensional theatrical poetry; indeed Lorca appears to have been the complete artist—poet, playwright, composer, recitalist, visual artist, director, actor, and so forth—from his very childhood. Nevertheless, it appears to me that Lorca's theatrical aesthetic that attained its most complete realization in his plays of the 1930s—not only in the so-called rural tragedies, but also the extraordinary experiments that are *As Five Years Pass* and *The Public*—evolved not from the narrative poetics of storytelling, nor the aesthetics of the commercial theater, but from the poetics of imagist poetry and that these poetics are to be found not only, and most obviously, in the "poetic" language of the plays but in their very dramaturgical construction.

While I have written elsewhere on supposed similarities and patent differences at various levels between the work of Lorca and the work of J.M. Synge and W.B. Yeats, what is interesting in this instant is their differences as writers of "poetic" theater.[2] As anyone growing up in Ireland and learning about the theater, my first encounter with a so-called "poetic" theater was that of Yeats and Synge. Despite the obvious quality of their stage work, it is testimony to the misconstruing of the notion of "poetic" theater as being theater where characters speak in verse or simply just florid language, that the only piece of any worth to emerge from the subsequent generation of "poetic" playwrights is Denis Johnston's satire on poetic theater, *The Old Lady Says No!*[3] For while there is a poetry to the language that Yeats and Synge would have their characters speak, and despite Yeats' flirtations with oriental models, the underlying dramaturgy of their stage-work always remains that of the well-made play—i.e., characters who embark upon a narrative that progresses by means of a Hegelian dialectic of Thesis-Antithesis-Synthesis. Whereas Lorca employs the logic of an imagist poem so that even when he appears to write a "well-made play," such as *Blood Wedding,* he underpins the more obvious narrative structure with a poetic structure. This structure takes the form of a journey through juxtaposed images and related emotions, the logic of which operates through the connections, disconnections, and oppositions. A model for this imagist dialectic might be: Image/emotion—Counterimage/counter-emotion—Symage/symotion. The journey may be that of one character as in *Dona Rosita*, several archetypal characters as in *As Five Years Pass* or an ever-changing kaleidoscope of characters, as in *The Public.* And this imagist logic is evident not only in the language of his plays, but also in every aspect of his plays' theatrical realization.

Pound's mini-Imagist (with a big I) masterstroke, if not masterpiece, "Papyrus" quoted above, is a perfectly distilled exemplum of this imagist (with a small i) logic at work. Like *The Public, As Five Years Pass,* and *Dona Rosita the Spinster,* "Papyrus" is a contemplation of time. Images and feelings are simply placed next to each other, the link between them not made explicit. The "narrative" momentum, at least the momentum that drives the reader through the poem, comes from these juxtapositions and from the reader's making of connections between these images. In fact, despite this little gem's brevity, this particular poem contains the subsumed structure of a three image / emotion play that in turn suggests three acts;

Spring—To hope
Too long—To long too long
Gongula—To die (with a possible resurrection)

And these acts function without the diversion of character and plot. Indeed, one could argue that it is the reader who is the central character.[4] What is also interesting about this little three image play is that the images and associated verbs echo exactly the formal progression of both *Dona Rosita* and *As Five Years Pass.*

And it is *As Five Years Pass* that concerns in this particular instant. This piece is less notorious and less notoriously difficult than *The Public,* but nevertheless, as Caridad Svich says in her note on the translation, Lorca saw it as one of his "impossible" plays. Stylistically it has been seen as a bridge between the near opacity of *The Public* and the seeming patent accessibility of the so-called rural tragedies.[5]

Unlike Pound's scrap of papyrus, there does appear to be some discernible storyline in *As Five Years Pass:* Young Man is prepared to wait for idealized love rather than accept actual love of Typist; Fiancée, having waited, wants actual physical love rather than the promised idealized love of Young Man; jilted Young Man searches out Typist as fallback and they realize that this is not the real thing and Young Man, already spiritually dead, dies.

Narratively each act revolves around a decision. Act 1: the Young Man's decision to wait for Fiancée and reject Typist—though in reality this never appears to be in doubt; Act 2: the Fiancée's decision to reject the Young Man and seek out Rugby Player—though yet again the girl has made it clear from the outset that she no longer desires the young man; Act 3: the mutual rejection of the Young Man and the Typist of the compromised love the other offers—though yet again there never really appears to be any chance this love will survive. Such, for what it's worth, are the narrative theses or "action" of the piece. However, to reduce or even consider this play solely in terms of narrative is to ignore the true means by which it actually works.

The fact that no character, apart from the servant John, possesses a name alerts us to the fact that this is not a narrative driven by psychologically verifiable characters; while the nonrealist set pieces such as the exchanges between the Dead Boy and the Cat, the Mannequin and the Young Man, and the Harlequin, Girl, and Clown, for example appear to operate beyond the requisites of the "story" as synopsized above or the prerequisites of a theses-led story in general as aptly described by David Mamet as "what the hero is trying to get" and therefore "what happens next."[6]

I believe this play is better conceived of as a theatrical poem that functions through images / emotion and counterimages / counteremotion that operate both with and beyond what is said. While I have described what "happens" in Act 1, this does not account for why Act 1 is as it is. The setting is a library, a repository of thoughts and feelings articulated and stored. An embittered and cynical old man and an idealistic young man talk of love. A dead boy enters; *"Thunder. Lights dim, and a stormy blue light envelops the stage. OLD MAN, YOUNG MAN, and FRIEND hide behind black screen covered with stars."* The dead boy appears to be one with nature, being almost interchangeable with the dead cat. Time telescopes in this play. Is the boy already dead? Or is he the boy who dies at the end of the act? Or is he, in fact, the young man's former self? Or all the above?

There are many more elements worthy of discussion in this act but let this brief description suffice for present purposes. To my mind the act is better understood as a kaleidoscope of male attitudes to love or, more exactly, passion. It could be read that all the male characters, apart from the Second Friend who does seem to express a different perspective, represent a heterosexual male attitude to love at various stages in a man's life. The Young Man is wholly oblivious to the physical and the actual reality of love while the Old Man seems bitter about all he has missed. Their locus is the library—the world of thoughts and feelings analyzed and articulated, but no longer felt. Hence the dead boy appears as a counterpoint to this vision of dominant male attitudes to passion and, as he does so, the library setting transmogrifies into the torrid nighttime setting described above. The dead boy also appears interchangeable with the cat and the cat is a "girl cat,"[7] which would suggest a much more fluid attitude to gender categories than the Young and Old Man possess. He is the man that might have been. He is at home with nature. He is unafraid of the potentially dangerous. But he is dead and we are returned to the library to conclude the act.

The act is concluded by the Second Friend. This character stands outside and reflects upon the scene. He discusses the burial of the boy. And, from this initial reflection, he reflects upon his own mortality; I've come back for my wings.

I've come back for my wings.
Let me come back.
I want to die while yesterday is upon me.
I want to die in the dawning. [8]

Hence, within the whole act as image of male attitudes and emotions toward passion at all ages, we have the internal imagist dialectic of image / emotion: man as passionless analyzer and delineator of the parameters of passion; counterimage / emotion: boy as essence of passion, and symage / symotion of man as poet of passion and mortality. This internal dialectic would also echo the broader dialectic of the three acts.

If Act 1 offers an image of heterosexual male attitudes to passion, Act 2 offers the counterimage of the woman's or the "other's" attitude. Notably the setting is the bedroom. The locus of passion. The Fiancée caresses the smoking, restless Rugby Player. His name, his action, his silence, and his title suggest sheer physicality. Once more this act breaks down into its own internal imagist dialectic. The counterimage to this depiction of physical passion is the young man himself. The whole tenor of the act shifts on his arrival to a rationalist argument. The symage / symotion at the end of the act is the Young Man dancing with a Mannequin that appears to be what his idealized long-waited-for love amounts to.

The final act as a whole offers a resolving symage to the play as well as having its own, internal dialectic. In the forest—a place so redolent to theater and psychoanalysis as a locus of sexuality—The Harlequin, Girl, and Clown play out a refracted / theatrical image of the relationships of the archetypal characters of the piece. The counterimage shows us the Young Man and the Typist attempting to inhabit this theatrico-sexual realm. Like theater itself, however, it is a transitory illusion;

YOUNG MAN: I've waited and died.

TYPIST: I died waiting

Gongula, with no chance of resurrection. The symage / symotion of the act and the play itself is once more the Library, the archive of thought and emotion. A card game, passion spent, the playing out of irrelevant card games—such is a life without passion and life without hope. The Young Man can barely maintain interest. The theatrical images shrivel and die with the Young Man's emotions. We are left with his death and the echo that is the echo of the representation itself.

"Don't apologize, don't explain!" the screenwriter Troy Kennedy Martin once said to me. On one level I have taken this to mean that if a work is of sufficient quality, it needs no justification extraneous to itself. However, I have latterly come to realize that quality work contains no internal justification either. A poem like "Papyrus" and plays like *As Five Years Pass* and *The Public* leave it to the reader or audience member to imagine the connections. The audience member or the reader must enter into the piece and become part of the creative process itself. It is more demanding than simply watching a Hollywood movie that explains how we are to read the links from A to B so we can get to "what happens next" with as little thought as possible. And twentieth-century audiences have been nurtured on such a diet of thoughtless "what happens next." It seems to me that if Lorca called these pieces "impossible theater" that the impossibility he detected in them was not so much in his ability to realize them or indeed in a theater company's ability to present them—though no doubt there have been many poor attempts—but more in the public's difficulty in submitting themselves to a poetic rather than a rationalist journey.

[1] E.Pound, "Papyrus", *Selected Poems,* Faber, London, 1928.

[2] See C.Teevan "Some Irish ReLorcations" in *Fire, Blood and the Alphabet; 100 Years of Federico García Lorca,* Durham Modern Language Series, Durham University, ed.s Dr. M.P.Thompson and S. Doggart, 1999.

[3] See D.Johnston,"The Old Lady Says No!" in *Collected Plays,* Cape, London, 1960 .

[4] Perhaps we might also infer from this that it is the audience member who is the hero of *The Public.* Is not the play named in his or her honor and is it not an heroic act to struggle through that particular journey?

[5] Though such occurrences as the talking moon of *Blood Wedding* should attest to a much less clear categories between the various plays.

[6] D. Mamet in "A Playwright in Hollywood," *A Whore's Profession, Notes and Essays,* Faber, London 1994, p. 163.

[7] From *As Five Years Pass.*

[8] From *As Five Years Pass.*

FROM THE TRUTH OF LIFE
TO THE LIFE OF TRUTH:
ASÍ QUE PASEN CINCO AÑOS (*AS FIVE YEARS PASS*)

By Paul Julian Smith

Así que pasen cinco años was first performed in Spain in Miguel Narros' production at Madrid's Teatro Eslava in 1978. Drama critics faithfully toed the academic line of interpretation, claiming like Manuel Gómez Ortiz in *Ya* that the Young Man is Federico and the action of the play is composed of his "internal monologue" ([no day given] September 1978) or like the anonymous critic of *ABC* that it depicts his "vertiginous introspections" (22 September 1978). *Ya* draws attention to a feature of José Hernández's set design that is relevant in this context: "tall cylinders which are [reminiscent of] tombs, chimneys, cerebral convolutions, skyscrapers, cypresses, with men standing on top of them like statues, men who start into movement when it is their turn to do so, men who exist and do not exist." The supposed unity of the action is thus reinforced by the flexible but single decor.

Critics inevitably stress the belatedness of the production, citing the almost half a century that has elapsed since the play's composition. And if they can no longer say, with Marcelle Auclair, "Federico is our youth," they invoke a shared experience of loss: Even Gómez Ortiz in the rightist *Ya* begins by confessing that his desire to see *Así que pasen cinco años* performed has lasted since he first read the play as a twenty year old in the 1950s. A kind of historical and cultural suspension has now been brought to a close. Enrique Llovet, writing on 21 September 1978 in *El País*, the new newspaper of the fragile democracy, begins: "The difficult, delicate, and delayed integration of Federico García Lorca's work into the framework of our contemporary theater now reaches its culmination and its closure ["cerramiento"] with the premiere, forty-seven years after it was written, of *Así que pasen cinco años*." The "enormity" of the delay does, however, have its compensations: Now we can see the totality of the experience of this difficult work and "the whole existence of a character" (the Young Man). As the headline puts it: "Lorca, All Lorca in One Play."[1]

When Narros restaged his production some ten years later at the Teatro Español ("two periods of five years," said the critics, suggesting like Freud that no period of time was indifferent), the reaction was more muted. Lorenzo López Sancho notes in *ABC* (30 April 1989) that, in a process of repetition and substitution, some of the cast recur, but playing different roles from the previous production: Thus Carlos Hipólito has shifted from Harlequin to Young Man; Melio Pedregal, from Clown to Old Man. Yet others, the critic notes, have been "devoured by time." The set design and performance style have also changed: Andrea d'Odorico's lavish sets "break the spatial unity" of the piece; the dialogue is "shouted" rather than spoken with the respect due its "subtle shading" ("texto matizado"); finally, the Italian-accented mask becomes in Manuela Vargas' performance a grotesquely distorted ("esperpéntica") Andaluza. The production thus "deuniversalizes" the play "leading it towards the aestheticizing *españolada*."

Eduardo Haro Tecglen concurs in *El País* (30 April 1989), in a notice entitled "Too Much" ("Demasiado"). While, unlike López Sancho, he is unconcerned with the "fidelity" of the production to the play or playwright (a question that he rightly considers "speculative" and "vain"), he finds everything excessive: the intensity of color, violence of sound, lushness of costume, and brilliance of lighting (this last by José Miguel López Sáez, who, Haro Tecglen tells us, came on stage after the premiere to take a bow). Moving from "a theater of text to a theater of spectacle," this is director's theater with a vengeance: Direction, decor, costume, effects, and lighting are dominant with García Lorca serving simply as a name before the title. Noting Narros' distinguished career as a director, Haro Tecglen claims that this is "more Narros than ever. Perhaps, also, too much so." Like the Parisian critics of thirty years before, then, Spaniards bemoan the excesses of this staging of *Así que pasen cinco años*; and both groups of critics, from their very different times and places, situate that excess in the ambiguous realm, so characteristic of approaches to García Lorca, between abstraction and folklore, universality and *españolada*.

Productions of *Así que pasen cinco años* thus seem to have a tendency toward performative excess, perhaps prompted by the troubling hermeticism of the text. It is tempting here to make a connection with Gide's insistence on the superfluity of the male, who represents that parade or spectacle, irreducible to reproduction, which (Gide claims) is the origin of both art and play.[2] Indeed, there is evidence for such a view in García Lorca himself. Refuting critical insistence on the supposed sterility of homosexuality, Auclair quotes a conversation with the poet and Rodríguez Rapún in which García Lorca praises the superiority of those who create art over those who simply procreate (p. 111). If we should reject that tendency to misogyny explicit in Gide's treatise and implicit in García Lorca's reported conversation, then still the male (the homosexual) supplement stands as a salutary corrective to that quest for the sexual essence of the subject we find in Schonberg's lethal "Corydonianism" and Ian Gibson's attempt to penetrate the private, a less prurient ambition, perhaps, but equally misguided.

I would suggest that the constant critical insistence that *Así que pasen cinco años* is a monologue and that its action is interiorized betrays a panic about the simple possibility of sexual relations between men that is itself underwritten by vulgarized psychoanalytic notions of homosexuality as narcissism. If we read the monologue as dialogue (Socratic or otherwise) and if we read sterile interiority as a fruitful relation to the other (a relation that is perhaps confirmed by the fantasies of procreation distributed throughout the play), then we would no longer collude with the mortal silence and solitude in which the Young Man, like the Director of *El público*, is condemned to death. Virgil's Eclogue III, the "amoebean" song in which two shepherds sing alternately the pleasures of both homo- and heterosexual love, stands as a classical model for such a dialogue, and one with which the García Lorca who cited so obliquely the name of Virgil may well have found sympathetic.

Rejected by the Fiancée, the Young Man cries: "You are nothing. You mean nothing. My treasure is lost. My love has no object." ("Tú no eres nada. Tú no significas nada. Es mi tesoro perdido. Es mi amor sin objeto."; II, pp. 271–72) This lost treasure might be read as Freud reads the jewel case in Dora's first dream, as the precious gift of the female genitals (p. 105). But it might also be seen as the "priceless though mutilated" object of analysis, a relic of past psychic time retrieved by the patient labor of the archeologist (p. 41). Faced with such valuable but imponderable objects, we can only defer meaning and not impose retrospectively an allegorical solution. Those critics who have insisted on turning the key of interpretation bear no relation to the Freud who insisted always on the role of condensation in the oneiric image. Thus, to take a motif familiar to García Lorca scholars, the black and white horses that are the precipitating cause (but not the simple or single origin) of

Little Hans's phobia are at once the adored mother whose childbirth preceded the horses' fall; the envied and loved father whose black moustache is a bridle; and the Hans himself who took such pleasure in movement ("I am a young horse"; p. 286). This plurality of identifications, simultaneous and sequential, so similar to those in Dora's case, requires extreme circumspection from any proponent of literary or psychic analysis. Moreover, the hermeticism of *Así que pasen cinco años*'s image repertoire suggests, paradoxically, that any hard distinction between real and symbolic is impossible to sustain: As feminist commentators have noted, when Freud claims to speak plainly ("J'appelle un chat un chat."; p. 82) he not only retreats into his non-native French; he also invokes, all unknowingly, a popular figurative name for the female genitalia.[3] I stress the fragility of the boundary between literal and symbolic, a boundary that both biographers and literary critics have so great an investment in preserving.

There is thus something to be said in favor of reticence. We have seen reticence in the brief, vertiginous dance of the Young Man and the First Friend; in Rodríguez Rapún's coded, classical allusion; in Marcelle Auclair's discreet refusal to impose meaning on the homosexuality she both saw and did not see; and (at its best) in Freud's analytical two-step, in which the analyst walks backwards in front of the analysand until both come to rest in the same place, albeit by following different routes. Even the aesthetic austerity of Gide's Corydon might serve as a lesson to French and to Spanish directors of *Así que pasen cinco años*, wallowing in the extravagance of the spectacle. In reticence we find the productivity of a postponement that is at once literary, hermeneutic, and libidinal. Reticence and postponement stake out the place (the time) of an elliptical drama without clear connections between its various fragments; of a meticulous interpretation that will be tolerant of unintelligibility; and of an intermittent desire whose goal lies tensely and tenderly suspended between autoerotism and object love.

García Lorca did not tell us his life story; and it would be naive to think that the publication of more missing personal letters, or indeed, more hitherto hidden manuscripts, would allow us to penetrate that mystery or fill its ever yawning gap. However, the persistent desire to read *Así que pasen cinco años* as a disguised autobiography responds to the fragmented nature of a process (of a life and a work) that like Dora's analysis was violently broken off. There is a third meaning of anamnesis that I have postponed until now. The anamnesis that is the recollection of things past and the patient's account of her medical history is also "that part of the Eucharistic canon in which the sacrifice of Christ is recalled."[4] García Lorca acolytes as varied as Schonberg,

Auclair, and Gibson have each left accounts of their retracing of the road to Víznar in a Calvary that is ever renewed. While I am sympathetic toward the role of repetition in preserving testimony to terror (most particularly in the case of an event without witnesses such as García Lorca's murder), I would suggest that it might be truer to the legacy of García Lorca's complex and critical texts to move from the truth of the life to the life of the truth. In other words, rather than imposing a fixed meaning on the past we should attempt (in Foucault's resonant phrase) "an archeology of the present," a process that, like the psychoanalytic case-study, will only be intelligible when it will have been completed. This need not imply a disavowal of those intense and varied emotions that so many have invested in the figure of the poet; after all, Freud and Breuer warn that, in the clinical context at least, recollection without affect is to no purpose (p. 57). Rather, in analytical two-step with García Lorca, one step behind and facing always back to front, we may finally find a way of remembering toward the future.

This essay is reprinted with permission from *The Theater of García Lorca: Text, Performance, Psychoanalysis* by Paul Julian Smith (New York: Cambridge University Press, 1998).

[1] "Lorca, todo Lorca, en una obra."

[2] *Corydon*, pp. 61, 66.

[3] Jane Gallop, "Keys to Dora," in Charles Bernheimer and Claire Kahane (eds.) *In Dora's Case: Feminism, Hysteria, Feminism* London: Virago, 1985), pp. 200–20 (p. 208).

[4] *Shorter Oxford English Dictionary* (Oxford: Clarendon, 1993), s.v. anamnesis.

Bill Torres as Friend and Carlos Orizondo as Young Man
from *As Five Years Pass*
Intar Theatre, New York, New York, 1998

photo by Sturgis Warner

AS FIVE YEARS PASS

Asi Que Pasen Cinco Años

A play by Federico García Lorca
in a new translation by Caridad Svich

This work was commissioned and produced by
Intar Hispanic American Arts Center, New York
as part of their "100 Years of Lorca" Festival
October 28–November 25, 1998
Director: Michael John Garces
Set Design: Van Santvoord, Costume Design: Katherine B. Roth
Light Design: Robert Williams

With cast as follows:

Servant/Father/Harlequin . . . . Oscar de la Fe Colón
Boy/Second Friend/First Player . . . . Yetta Gottesman
Typist/Mannequin/Girl . . . . Mercedes Herrero
Fiancee/Third Player . . . . Sol Miranda
Young Man . . . . Carlos Orizondo
Old Man . . . . Carlos Rafart
Friend/Rugby Player/Clown/Second Player . . . . Bill Torres
Cat/Maid/Mask . . . . Marilyn Torres

As Five Years Pass is both a "legend of time," as Federico García Lorca subtitled the play, and a "dream play," with roots in the French symbolist theater of the 1920s and 30s. It is a deeply personal play where Lorca fuses images from his childhood with purely theatrical images from his imagination, drawing inevitably as any poet does, from his poetry and earlier texts.

The play is divided into three distinct acts, which function almost as three different mini-plays, each with its own tone and pace. The first act set in the Library is not only the beginning of the play but the foundation of the play—all the later strands spring from this act.

It could be argued that this play, written five years before Lorca's untimely death, was his own "dance with death," and that the elastic sense of time and space that Lorca gives the play is a way of presenting the fluid nature of not only time, but our perception of it, as well as a desire to incorporate and distill the totality of his work into one piece of art.

Certainly, it is a play of premonitions, and startling surprises, which upon further review, one realizes are not surprises at all but moments of recognition—remembering what has been forgotten in the mind.

Although *As Five Years Pass* is autobiographical in nature, it would be reductive to view it only through this authorial prism, for what the text offers is a visionary theatrical experience that is both modernist in sensibility (as befitting its time) but also surprisingly contemporary in the way it orchestrates its delicate, emotive scenario.

Lorca posited this play, along with *El Público* and his earlier miniature plays *Buster Keaton Takes a Walk, Chimera,* and *The Maiden, The Sailor, and The Student,* as his venture into the creation of an "impossible theater," which he considered his "true" theater—a reflection of his authentic writing voice.

It is this "impossible" theater, which takes its cue from the "esperpentos" of Lorca's pre-cursor Valle-Inclán, which, more so than his famous rural tragedies, places Lorca as the forerunner of a boldly innovative theatrical tradition that is democratic in its mix of styles and sensibillities—a "hybrid" theater that has shaped a generation of dramatists from Iberia to the Americas to western Europe and the Balkans.

With this translation, I have sought to liberate Lorca's voice into the English language in a manner that is both faithful in letter and spirit to the original in all its deliberate obfuscations, but also to capture the lucid wakefulness of Lorca's writing. A thinly veiled expression of heartbreak and loss,

As Five Years Pass is a meta-theatrical investigation into the dreams and nightmares of the poetic heart.

As a dramatist deeply influenced by Lorca in my own work, the dialogue across time, which this kind of translation experience provides, has allowed me to explore the interior of Lorca's imagination with a privilege that is uncommon to a reader or witness of the work on stage. The breath and tone of Lorca that lives inside the language of his work is playful and profound, and the translation process has illuminated for me the powerfully intricate and mysterious nature of collaboration.

As Five Years Pass marks the beginning of Lorca's mature work as a dramatist. Written in 1931 and unproduced in his lifetime, it is a work that stands with *El Público* as a tantalizing glimpse into the kind of theater Lorca would have given us had not the politics of a brutal war stopped his vision short.

Caridad Svich

CHARACTERS

Act One: The Library:
- YOUNG MAN
- OLD MAN
- BOY
- CAT
- SERVANT JOHN
- FRIEND
- SECOND FRIEND
- THE TYPIST

Act Two: The Bedroom:
- FIANCÉE
- RUGBY PLAYER
- MAID
- FATHER
- MANNEQUIN

Act Three: The Forest and The Library:
- HARLEQUIN
- GIRL
- CLOWN
- MASK
- FIRST PLAYER
- SECOND PLAYER
- THIRD PLAYER
- Two silent MASKS, and Two silent SERVANTS.

Primary roles may be cast with 4 women and 4 men, with roles doubled as suggested:
- YOUNG MAN (M)
- OLD MAN (M)
- TYPIST/MANNEQUIN/GIRL (F)
- MAID/MASK/CAT (F)
- BOY/SECOND FRIEND/FIRST PLAYER (F)
- FRIEND/RUGBY PLAYER/CLOWN/SECOND PLAYER (M)
- SERVANT JOHN/FATHER/HARLEQUIN (M)
- FIANCÉE/THIRD PLAYER (F)

ACT ONE

Library. The YOUNG MAN is seated. He wears blue pajamas. The OLD MAN wears a gray morning coat. He has a white beard and large gold-rimmed spectacles. He is also seated.

YOUNG MAN: You're not surprised.

OLD MAN: Sorry…

YOUNG MAN: It's always the same.

OLD MAN: *(Inquisitive and kind.)* Really?

YOUNG MAN: Yes.

OLD MAN: It's that…

YOUNG MAN: I remember…

OLD MAN: *(Laughs.)* I always remember.

YOUNG MAN: I…

OLD MAN: *(With longing.)* Go on…

YOUNG MAN: I would save the sweets for later.

OLD MAN: Later. Really? They taste better later. I too…

YOUNG MAN: I remember one day…

OLD MAN: *(Interrupting vehemently.)* I do so like the word *remember.* It's a green word, a succulent word. Endless drops of cool water spring from it.

YOUNG MAN: *(Cheerful and trying to convince himself.)* Yes, yes, of course. You are right. It's important to stave off any notion of ruin. With those terribly stripped walls. Many times I have gotten up at midnight to pull the weeds from the garden. I don't want weeds in my house, or dilapidated furniture either.

OLD MAN: Exactly. You must not remember even the dilapidated furniture, only…

YOUNG MAN: Only those things which are alive, burning with blood, with profiles unmarred.

OLD MAN: Very well. That is to say *(Lowering his voice.)* one has to remember, only one should remember before.

YOUNG MAN: Before?

OLD MAN: *(With an air of secrecy.)* Yes, one must remember into tomorrow.

YOUNG MAN: *(Absorbed.)* Into tomorrow.

(The clock strikes six. The TYPIST crosses the stage, crying silently.)

OLD MAN: Six o'clock.

YOUNG MAN: Yes, six and awfully hot. *(He rises.)* The sky promises a beautiful storm. Full of gray clouds…

OLD MAN: So you…? I was a great friend of that family. Especially of the father. He was an astronomer. He's doing well with astronomy, eh? And her?

YOUNG MAN: I don't know her well. But it's not important. I think she loves me.

OLD MAN: Of course!

YOUNG MAN: They went on a long trip. It almost made me happy…

OLD MAN: Did her father come?

YOUNG MAN: Never! It's not possible at the moment… For reasons I cannot explain. Until five years pass.

OLD MAN: *(Happily.)* That's good!

YOUNG MAN: *(Serious.)* Why do you say that?

OLD MAN: Because… *(Looking about the room.)* Is this a nice place?

YOUNG MAN: No.

OLD MAN: Doesn't taking leave bother you? All that is to transpire, the arrangements, what is to come right now…?

YOUNG MAN: Yes, yes. Don't speak to me of it.

OLD MAN: What's happening in the street?

YOUNG MAN: Noise. Always noise, dust, heat, horrible smells. It bothers me that the sounds of the street come into my house.

(A long wail is heard. Pause.)

YOUNG MAN: John, close the window.

(A subtle SERVANT, who walks on tiptoe, closes the window.)

OLD MAN: She…is young?

YOUNG MAN: Very young. Fifteen years old.

OLD MAN: Fifteen years she has lived. Fifteen is she. But why not say she is fifteen snows, fifteen breezes, fifteen twilights? Why don't you dare leave? Fly? Hang your love across the entire sky?

YOUNG MAN: *(Covers his face with his hands.)* I love her too much!

OLD MAN: *(Rising, with energy.)* Oh to say: She is fifteen roses, fifteen wings, fifteen grains of sand. Do you not dare concentrate, transform the love in your heart into something wounded and small?

YOUNG MAN: You want to take her away from me. But I know your game. You have only to look at a live insect in the palm of your hand, or look at the ocean in the afternoon, paying close watch to the shape of each wave to make this open wound, this sore we carry in our chest dissolve into tears. I am in love, and I want to be in love, as in love as she is with me. For that I can wait five years, so that we may make love in the night—her braids of light around my neck, while the rest of the world goes dark.

OLD MAN: May I remind you that your girlfriend…does not have braids?

YOUNG MAN: *(Irritable.)* I know. She cut them off without my permission, naturally, and this… *(Anguished.)* she changes her image. *(Vigorously.)* I know she doesn't have braids. *(Furiously.)* Why have you reminded me? *(With sadness.)* But as these five years pass, she will have them again.

OLD MAN: *(With enthusiasm.)* And more beautiful than ever. They will be such braids…

YOUNG MAN: *(Cheerfully.)* They are, they are.

OLD MAN: They are braids in whose perfume you may live without need of bread or water.

YOUNG MAN: I think too much…!

OLD MAN: You dream too much.

YOUNG MAN: What?

OLD MAN: I think so much I…

YOUNG MAN: That my flesh is raw. Deep inside me. Burning.

OLD MAN: *(Offers a drink.)* Drink.

YOUNG MAN: Thank you. If I start to think of the girl, my girl…

OLD MAN: Say my "fiancée." I dare you!

YOUNG MAN: No.

OLD MAN: Why not?

YOUNG MAN: Fiancée… You know why not. If I say "fiancée" I see her shrouded in a sky held together by large braids of snow. No, she is not my fiancée, not my bride. She is my girl, my little girl.

OLD MAN: Go on, go on.

YOUNG MAN: If I start to think of her! I start to draw her. I make her move white and alive. But all of a sudden who changes her nose, breaks her teeth? Who turns her into just another tattered woman that crosses through my mind as if she was looking at herself in a carnival mirror?

OLD MAN: Who? It's unbelievable to me that you would say such. What is before us changes more than what we see in the distance, what crosses the back of our minds. The water that comes from the river is completely different from that which leaves the river's mouth. Who can recall a map of the desert sands that is truly exact…? Or the face of a friend that truly matches your image of them?

YOUNG MAN: Yes, yes. What is inside us is more alive than what is on the outside, even though everything changes. The last time I saw her I could not look at her closely because she had two wrinkles across her forehead that filled her face and made her look sallow, old, as if she had suffered a great deal in her life. I needed to keep my distance from her so I could focus on her. Yes. That is the word. Focus her in my heart.

OLD MAN: Tell me, was she about to surrender herself to you completely at the moment in which you saw her old and wrinkled?

YOUNG MAN: Yes.

OLD MAN: *(Exalted.)* And if in that moment she would have confessed to you that she had betrayed you, that she did not love you, would her wrinkles not have erased, would she not have seemed to possess the most delicate skin, a skin of soft rose petals brushing against your cheek?

YOUNG MAN: *(Exalted.)* Yes.

OLD MAN: And you would have not loved her more, precisely because of her confession?

YOUNG MAN: Yes, yes.

OLD MAN: Then? Ha, ha!

YOUNG MAN: Then… it is very difficult to go on living.

OLD MAN: That is why you must go from one thing to the next until you lose yourself. If she is fifteen years old, she could have fifteen twilights or fifteen skies. Things are more alive inside than out there in the open air exposed to death. That is why we must…not go…or wait. Because to do anything else is to die right now, and it is better to think that tomorrow we will once again see the one hundred horns of gold with which the sun pushes away the clouds at dawn.

YOUNG MAN: *(Extending his hand.)* Thank you! Thank you! For everything.

OLD MAN: I will return.

(The TYPIST appears.)

YOUNG MAN: Did you finish typing the letters?

TYPIST: *(Teary-eyed.)* Yes, sir.

OLD MAN: *(To YOUNG MAN.)* What's wrong with her?

TYPIST: I wish to leave this house.

OLD MAN: That is easy enough, no?

YOUNG MAN: *(Worried.)* You will see.

TYPIST: I want to leave and I cannot.

YOUNG MAN: *(Sweetly.)* It is not I who detains her. You know I cannot do anything. I have told you many times you should wait, but you…

TYPIST: I do not wait. Why should I?

OLD MAN: Why not? To wait is to go on believing, to go on living.

TYPIST: I do not wait because I do not want to, I do not care to, and yet, I cannot leave this place.

YOUNG MAN: You always end up not giving any reasons to anybody.

TYPIST: What reasons should I give? There is only one reason and it is this…that I love you. Don't be alarmed, sir! I've always loved him. When he was a child *(To OLD MAN.)* I would watch him from my balcony as he played. One day he fell and his knee was bleeding. Remember? *(To YOUNG MAN.)* I still remember that blood like a red serpent trembling in my bosom.

OLD MAN: That is not right. Blood dries and what is past is past.

TYPIST: What fault have I, sir? I can't help it. *(To YOUNG MAN.)* I beg you to give me notice. I want to leave this house.

YOUNG MAN: Very well. But it's not my fault either. Anyhow, you know perfectly well I don't belong to anyone. You can leave.

TYPIST: *(To OLD MAN.)* You hear him? He is throwing me out of his house. He does not want me here.

(She exits, crying.)

OLD MAN: *(To YOUNG MAN.)* That woman is dangerous.

YOUNG MAN: I wish I could love her like I wish I could become thirsty at the sight of a fountain. I wish…

OLD MAN: Nonsense! What would you do tomorrow? Eh? Think. Only tomorrow!

(The FRIEND enters with great noise.)

FRIEND: This is such a silent house. And for what? Give me water with anisette and ice.

(The OLD MAN leaves.)

FRIEND: Or a cocktail.

YOUNG MAN: I hope you don't intend to wreck my furniture.

FRIEND: A man alone, a serious man, and in such hot weather!

YOUNG MAN: Won't you sit down?

FRIEND: *(Grabs YOUNG MAN by the arm and spins.)* Heigh, ho, hooray, goes St. John's little flame.

YOUNG MAN: Let me be. I'm not in the mood for jokes.

FRIEND: Ohhh! Who was that old man? A friend of yours? And where in this house are the portraits of all the girls you've slept with? Look *(Drawing near.)* I am going to grab you by your lapels, I'm going to paint your sallow cheeks with rouge…or rub them hard, like this.

YOUNG MAN: *(Annoyed.)* Get away from me!

FRIEND: And with a cane, I will toss you out into the street.

YOUNG MAN: And what would I do in the street? You'd like that, eh? It's hard enough just listening to the racket of the cars and of the lost souls wailing at all hours.

FRIEND: *(Sits and stretches himself on the sofa.)* Ah! Oh! I, on the other hand…Yesterday I had three girls, and the day before that, I had two, and today, one. Well… now I have none, because I do not have time. I was with a girl… Ernestine. You want to meet her?

YOUNG MAN: No.

FRIEND: Noo and with flourish! But if you saw her, she has such a figure…! No, actually Matilda has a better figure. *(Impetuously.)* Oh, dear God! *(Jumps up, then falls onto the sofa.)* Look, she's got a figure to fit anyone's arms, and she's so fragile that all you want to do is have a small silver ax in your hand so you can cut her up into little slices.

YOUNG MAN: *(Distracted.)* Then I will go upstairs.

FRIEND: *(Bellyflops onto sofa.)* I don't have time, I don't have time for anything, I get run over by everything. Just imagine. I make a date with Ernestine. She wraps her deep black braids around me tight, and then… *(The YOUNG MAN drums his fingers on the table impatiently.)*

YOUNG MAN: You do not let me think!

FRIEND: But you don't have to think! Well, I'm going. No matter… what I do… *(Looks at clock.)* The hour's gone; it's horrible, isn't it? It's always the same. I don't have time. I'm sorry. I went out with a terribly ugly woman, but admirable nonetheless, one of those dark-skinned women, who think nothing of acting their age. I like her *(Throwing a cushion up into the air.)* because she looks like a hussy.

YOUNG MAN: Enough!

FRIEND: Don't get all bent out of shape. A virtuous woman can be incredibly ugly, and a hussy can be beautiful. And vice versa… what do you say? *(Serves himself a cocktail.)*

YOUNG MAN: Nothing…

FRIEND: You want to tell me what's the matter with you?

YOUNG MAN: Nothing's the matter. Don't you know me by now?

FRIEND: No. I don't understand you. But I can't take everything seriously. *(Laughs.)* I'll greet you like the Eskimo do. *(Rubs his nose against the YOUNG MAN's nose in an Eskimo kiss.)*

YOUNG MAN: Stop it.

FRIEND: *(Tickles YOUNG MAN.)* Come on, laugh.

YOUNG MAN: *(Laughs.)* Scoundrel.

(THEY wrestle.)

FRIEND: I'll flatten you out.

YOUNG MAN: I can handle you.

FRIEND: Caught you.

> (*FRIEND grabs YOUNG MAN's head between his legs and hits him. The OLD MAN enters in a somber mood.*)

OLD MAN: With your permission... (*YOUNG MAN and his FRIEND stand.*) Excuse me... (*Looking at YOUNG MAN with brio.*) I will forget my hat.

FRIEND: What?

OLD MAN: (*Angrily.*) Yes, sir. I will forget my hat... (*Between his teeth.*) That is to say, I have forgotten my hat.

FRIEND: Ahhhh...!

> (*The sound of glass breaking.*)

YOUNG MAN: (*Raising his voice.*) John. Close the windows.

FRIEND: A small storm. I hope it's strong!

YOUNG MAN: Well, I don't want to hear it! (*Raising his voice.*) I want everything closed.

FRIEND: Thunder. You've no choice but to hear it.

YOUNG MAN: Oh no.

FRIEND: Oh yes.

YOUNG MAN: I don't care what happens outside. This is my house, and I won't let anyone in.

OLD MAN: (*To FRIEND, indignantly.*) It's an irrefutable fact!

> (*Distant thunder is heard.*)

YOUNG MAN: (*Shouting.*) Not now. Not now!

OLD MAN: Bravo...!

FRIEND: Open the window! I'm hot.

OLD MAN: We'll open it!

YOUNG MAN: Later!

FRIEND: Wait a minute...Are you telling me...

> (*More thunder. Lights dim, and a stormy blue light envelopes the stage. OLD MAN, YOUNG MAN, and FRIEND hide behind a black screen covered with stars. The dead BOY appears from a door stage left with a CAT. The BOY is dressed in white, as if for his First Communion, with a crown of white roses on his head. His eyes and lips, dry as lilies, stand out in his white waxen face. In his hand, a curved wax candle, and a large ribbon of golden flowers. The CAT is blue with two enormous bloodstains on its small white-gray chest and head. They walk toward the audience. The BOY holds the CAT by one of its legs.*)

CAT: Meow.

BOY: Hiss…

CAT: Meow.

BOY: Take my white handkerchief.

    Take my white crown.

    Do not cry anymore.

CAT: The open wounds on my back,

    Where the children beat me, hurt.

BOY: My heart also hurts.

CAT: Why does it hurt, child, why?

BOY: Because it does not work.

    The nightingale of my pillow

    Slowly stopped yesterday.

    Such noise. If you would have seen it…! They put me

    in front of the window with these roses on my head.

CAT: And what could you hear?

BOY: I could hear

    Bubbles and bees round my bed.

    They tied my hands together. Badly done!

    The children looked at me through the window.

    And a man with a hammer slowly nailed

    Paper stars into my coffin.

    (He crosses his hands.)

BOY: The angels did not come. No, Tomcat.

CAT: Stop calling me Tomcat.

BOY: No?

CAT: I'm a girl cat.

BOY: You're a girl cat?

CAT: *(Affectionately.)* You should've known.

BOY: How?

CAT: By my silvery voice.

BOY: *(Gallantly.)* Won't you sit down?

CAT: Yes. I'm hungry.

BOY: I'll go see if I can find you a rat.

    (The BOY begins to look under the chairs. The CAT sits on a stool, trembling.)

BOY: Don't eat it all. Just one of its feet,

    Because you are very sick.

CAT: The boys threw ten stones at me.

BOY: They weigh as much as the roses
    That imprisoned my throat last night.
    Would you like one?
    (He tears a rose from his head.)
CAT: *(Cheerfully.)* Yes, I'd like one.
BOY: With your wax stains, white rose,
    And your broken moon's eye, you seem like
    A gazelle who has fainted beneath the windows.
    (He places the rose on the CAT.)
CAT: What did you used to do?
BOY: Play, and you?
CAT: Play!
    I would walk on the roof, snub-nosed cat,
    Pressing my nose against the flats;
    And in the morning
    I would look for the fishes in the water,
    And at noon
    I would sleep against the wall beneath the bush.
BOY: And at night?
CAT: *(Emphatically.)* I would walk alone.
BOY: With no one.
CAT: Through the woods.
BOY: *(Happily.)* I would too. Oh, cheap, snub-nosed cat.
    I would go to eat apples and blackberries
    And then to church with the other children
    To play the "goat."
CAT: What is the "goat?"
BOY: To suck the nails off the doors.
CAT: Did they taste good?
BOY: No, Cat! It was like sucking coins.
    (Distant thunder.)
BOY: Oh! Wait! They're not here yet? I'm afraid,
    You know? I ran away from home.
    (Cries.)
BOY: I don't want them to bury me.
    Lilies and glass adorn my coffin;
    it is better that I sleep
    by the reeds of the river.
    I don't want them to bury me. No!

(He grabs CAT by the leg.)

CAT: They're going to bury us? When?

BOY: Tomorrow.

>In a couple of dark holes.
>
>Everyone cries. Everyone grows silent.
>
>But they leave. I saw them.
>
>And afterwards, you know what happens?

CAT: What happens?

BOY: They come and eat us.

CAT: Who?

BOY: The lizard and his wife,

>And all their little kids, and there are many.

CAT: And what do they eat?

BOY: Our faces, our fingers

>*(Lowering his voice.)*

BOY: And our peepees.

CAT: *(Offended.)* I don't have a peepee.

BOY: *(With vigor.)* Cat!

>They will eat your feet and mustache.
>
>*(Very distant thunder.)*

BOY: Let's go. We will go from house to house

>Until we come to where the seahorses graze.
>
>It is not heaven. It is hard earth
>
>Where crickets sing,
>
>Where the grass sways,
>
>Where the clouds rise,
>
>And the slingshots fling
>
>Rocks and stones
>
>And the wind is like a sword.
>
>I want to be a boy! A boy!
>
>*(He heads to the stage right door.)*

CAT: The door is closed.

>Let's take the stairs.

BOY: They'll see us on the stairs.

CAT: Wait.

BOY: They're coming to bury us!

CAT: Let's go through the window.

BOY: We'll never see the light,

>Nor the clouds rise,

Nor the crickets in the grass,

Nor the sword-like wind.

(Crosses his hands.)

BOY: Oh sunflower!

Oh sunflower of fire!

Oh sunflower!

CAT: Oh carnation of the sun.

BOY: Shut out by the sky.

Only mountains and oceans of coal,

And a dove lying dead in the sand

With her wings clipped and a flower in her beak.

(They sing.)

BOY: "From the flower an olive,

From the olive a lime..."

How does it go...? I don't know how it goes...?

CAT: Oh sunflower!

Oh sunflower of the dawn!

BOY: Oh carnation of the sun!

(Lights dim. The BOY and CAT hold onto each other, groping.)

CAT: The light's gone. Where are you?

BOY: Quiet.

CAT: Will the lizards come now, boy?

BOY: No.

CAT: You've found a way out?

(CAT draws near stage right door. A hand appears, pulling her inside.)

CAT: *(From inside.)* Boy! Boy! Boy!

(Anguished.)

CAT: Boy, boy!

(BOY moves toward her voice with terror, stopping after each step.)

BOY: *(Softly.)* She's disappeared.

A hand has taken her.

It must have been God's hand.

Don't bury me. Give me a couple minutes...

While I strip the petals off this flower.

(He pulls flower from his head and strips its petals.)

BOY: I will go alone, very slowly,

And you will let me look at the sun...

And with a ray of light I will be content.

(Continues to strip petals off the flower.)

BOY: Yes, no. Yes, no. Yes.

VOICE: No, no.

BOY: I always said no.

> (A hand appears, and carries off the BOY, who faints. As the BOY disappears, the LIGHTS come up to their original intensity. From behind the screen, the OLD MAN, YOUNG MAN, and FRIEND quickly appear. They are flushed and quite agitated. The YOUNG MAN has a blue fan in his hand; the OLD MAN, a black fan, and the FRIEND, a bright red fan. They fan themselves.)

OLD MAN: Well, there will be more later.

YOUNG MAN: Yes, later.

FRIEND: Quite enough for now. I think you won't be able to escape the storm.

VOICE: (From outside.) My son! My son!

YOUNG MAN: Sir, what an afternoon it has been! John, who's shouting thus?

> (SERVANT enters on tiptoe, speaking in a soft voice.)

SERVANT: The porter's son has died. They will take his body to be buried now. His mother cries.

FRIEND: It's only natural!

OLD MAN: Yes, yes. But what's past is past.

FRIEND: It's barely passing now.

> (They argue. The SERVANT crosses the stage, is about to exit stage left when.)

SERVANT: Sir. Would you be so kind as to let me have the keys to your bedroom?

YOUNG MAN: What for?

SERVANT: The children killed a cat, and flung it onto the garden awning. It will be necessary to remove the animal.

YOUNG MAN: (Bothered.) Here. (To OLD MAN.) Can't you do something about it?

OLD MAN: I do not care to.

FRIEND: You're lying. You do care. It is I who does not care, because I know for a fact that snow is cold and fire burns.

OLD MAN: (Ironically.) That depends.

FRIEND: (To YOUNG MAN.) He's lying to you.

> (The OLD MAN looks at the FRIEND with intensity, crushing his hat.)

YOUNG MAN: (Forcefully.) He doesn't influence me in the least. I am who I am. But you cannot understand what it's like to wait for a woman for five years, filled with a burning love that only grows stronger every day.

FRIEND: You don't need to wait!

YOUNG MAN: You think I can overcome the material world, the obstacles that arise in my path, and become greater without causing anyone any pain?

FRIEND: You have to think of yourself first. Before anyone else.

YOUNG MAN: As I wait, the knot unties itself, and fruit ripens.

FRIEND: I prefer to eat my fruit green, or better yet, I like to cut its blossom, so I can wear it on my lapel.

OLD MAN: That is not true!

FRIEND: You're too old to know about such things!

OLD MAN: *(Severely.)* I have fought all my life to bring out the light in even the darkest of places. And when people have tried to wring the dove's neck, I have stopped their hands, and have helped the dove fly again.

FRIEND: And, naturally, the hunter has died of hunger!

YOUNG MAN: Blessed hunger be!

(From a door stage left, the SECOND FRIEND appears. He is dressed in white, in an impeccable wool suit. He wears white shoes and gloves. If a young male actor cannot be found to play this role, then it should be played by a girl. The suit is exaggeratedly cut, with enormous blue buttons, and a vest and a tie of ruffled lace.)

SECOND FRIEND: Blessed indeed, when there is toasted bread, olive oil, and sound sleep afterwards. Deep sleep. That never ends. I have heard you.

YOUNG MAN: *(Surprised.)* How did you get in here?

SECOND FRIEND: I found a way. Through the window. Two boys helped me, good friends of mine. I met them when I was very young. They pushed me in by my feet. A heavy rain is going to fall…but what a lovely heavy rain it was last year. The light was so dim that my hands turned yellow. *(To OLD MAN.)* Do you remember?

OLD MAN: *(Sourly.)* I remember nothing.

SECOND FRIEND: *(To FRIEND.)* And you?

FRIEND: *(Somberly.)* Neither.

SECOND FRIEND: I was very young, but I remember everything with great detail.

FRIEND: Look…

SECOND FRIEND: That is why I do not want to see it this time. Rain can be so beautiful. When I was in school, it would come in through the schoolyards and would cover the walls with stars, with tiny naked women, that lived inside each drop. Have you never seen this? When I was five years old... no, when I was two... I lie. I was only a year old. It's a beautiful thing, isn't it? One year I caught one of these little women of the rain in my hand and placed her in a fishbowl for two days.

FRIEND: *(Sarcastically.)* And did she grow?

SECOND FRIEND: No. She became smaller and smaller, more a girl than a woman. As she should have, as was right. Until all that was left of her was one drop of water. And she sang a song...

> I've come back for my wings.
> Let me come back.
> I want to die in the dawning.
> I want to die while yesterday is upon me.
> I've come back for my wings.
> Let me come back.
> I want to die in the spring.
> I want to die away
> From the sea...

Which is precisely what I sing at all hours.

OLD MAN: *(To YOUNG MAN, irritably.)* He's completely mad.

SECOND FRIEND: *(Overhearing.)* Mad? Because I do not want to be full of wrinkles, and aches and pains like yourself? Because I want to live my life, but it is taken away from me? I do not know you, sir. I do not want to have anything to do with people like you.

FRIEND: *(Drinking.)* You're just afraid of death.

SECOND FRIEND: No. Just now, before coming in here, I saw a child that was about to be buried as the first drops of rain were beginning to come down. That is how I would like to be buried. In a small coffin. All of you can go weather the storm. But my face is mine. And it is being taken away from me. I used to be tender. I used to sing. And now there is a man, an old man *(To OLD MAN.)* like you, who wanders inside me with two or three masks at the ready. *(Pulls out a mirror and looks at himself.)* But not yet. I still see myself climbing the cherry trees...with that gray suit... A gray suit with silver anchors... My God! *(He covers his face with his hands.)*

OLD MAN: Suits tatter, anchors rust, but we go on.

SECOND FRIEND: Oh, please, don't talk like that!

OLD MAN: *(With enthusiasm.)* Houses collapse.

FRIEND: *(Energetically, with a defensive air.)* Houses do not collapse.

OLD MAN: *(Undaunted.)* The eyes dim, and a razor-sharp sickle reaps the reeds along the riverbanks.

SECOND FRIEND: Of course! But much time must pass before that happens.

OLD MAN: On the contrary. It has already passed.

SECOND FRIEND: Behind us, all is still. How is it you do not know this? All you have to do is slowly wake everything. On the other hand, in four or five years, we will all fall into a well that is already waiting for us.

OLD MAN: *(Furious.)* Silence!

YOUNG MAN: *(Trembling before the OLD MAN.)* Have you heard him?

OLD MAN: I have heard too much.

(OLD MAN exits quickly through stage right door.)

YOUNG MAN: *(After him.)* Where are you going? Why do you run off like that? Wait!

(YOUNG MAN exits after OLD MAN.)

SECOND FRIEND: *(Shrugs.)* Well. Just like an old man. You, on the other hand, haven't said a word.

FRIEND: *(Who has stopped drinking.)* No.

SECOND FRIEND: Drinking's enough for you.

FRIEND: *(Serious; with honesty.)* I do what I want, what I like. I haven't asked for your opinion.

SECOND FRIEND: *(Fearfully.)* Yes, yes. I wouldn't tell you anything…

(SECOND FRIEND sits in an armchair with his legs drawn. FRIEND quickly downs all the drinks, not leaving a drop, and hitting himself in the forehead as if he has remembered something, exits quickly through stage left door. SECOND FRIEND rests his head on the armchair. The SERVANT appears from stage right, walking on tiptoe, his manner refined. It starts to rain.)

SECOND FRIEND: The downpour. *(He looks at his hands.)* What a horrible light. *(He falls asleep.)*

YOUNG MAN: *(Entering.)* Tomorrow he will come back. I need him. *(He sits.)*

(The TYPIST appears. She carries a suitcase. She crosses the stage. Midstage, she turns around quickly.)

TYPIST: Did you call me?

YOUNG MAN: *(Closing his eyes.)* No. No, I did not call you.

(The TYPIST begins to exit, looking at the YOUNG MAN anxiously, waiting for his call.)

TYPIST: *(At the door.)* Do you need me?

YOUNG MAN: *(Closing his eyes.)* No. No, I do not need you.

(The TYPIST exits.)

SECOND FRIEND: *(In dream.)* I've come back for my wings.

> Let me come back.
>
> I want to die while yesterday is upon me.
>
> I want to die in the dawning.
>
> *(Rain.)*

YOUNG MAN: It's getting late, John. Turn on the lights. What time is it?

SERVANT: *(Willfully.)* It is six o'clock sharp, sir.

YOUNG MAN: Very well.

SECOND FRIEND: *(In dream.)* I've come back for my wings.

> Let me come back again.
>
> I want to die in the spring.
>
> I want to die away
>
> from the sea.
>
> *(YOUNG MAN gently drums his fingers on the table. Slow curtain.)*

END OF ACT ONE

ACT TWO

Turn-of-the-century style bedroom. Extreme furniture. Large draperies full of pleats and tassels. Clouds and angels are painted on the walls. In the center of the room there is a bed framed with plumage and assorted fabric hangings. To the left there is a dressing table held up by angels with branches of electric lights in their hands. The balconies are open, and the moonlight shines through them. From Offstage, a car horn is heard honking furiously. The FIANCÉE jumps out of bed wearing a splendid robe decorated with lace and enormous rose-colored bows. Her robe has a long train. Her hair is all in ringlets.

FIANCÉE: *(Going to the balcony.)* Come up.
   (A car horn is heard.)
FIANCÉE: You must. My fiancé—the old one, the poet—is on his way, and
   I need to lean on you.
   (The RUGBY PLAYER enters through the balcony; he wears knee pads and a helmet. He carries a bag full of cigars, which he lights and extinguishes incessantly.)
FIANCÉE: Come in. I haven't seen you for two days.
   (They embrace. The RUGBY PLAYER does not speak. He only smokes and crushes the cigar butts with his foot. He seems to be possessed of a great vitality. He embraces the FIANCÉE impetuously.)
FIANCÉE: Today you have kissed me differently. You always change, my
   love. Yesterday I did not see you, you know? But I did see your horse.
   He was beautiful: white with golden hooves gleaming through the hay
   in the mangers.
   (She sits on the sofa that is at the foot of the bed.)
FIANCÉE: But you are more beautiful. Because you are like a dragon.
   (She embraces him.)
FIANCÉE: I think I am going to break in your arms, because I am weak,
   because I am small, because I am like the frost, because I am like a tiny
   guitar burned by the sun, but you do not break me.
   (The RUGBY PLAYER blows smoke in her face.)
FIANCÉE: *(Running her hand down his neck.)* Behind all this shadow there
   is a great silver bridge that spans and defends me, for I am as tiny as a
   button, as tiny as a bee who enters suddenly into the throne room. Isn't
   that true? Isn't that true? I will go along with you.
   (She rests her head on the RUGBY PLAYER's chest.)

FIANCÉE: Dragon, my dragon! How many hearts do you have? There is a
raging river inside your chest where I will drown. I will drown myself
(She looks at him.) and you will run away and leave me dead on the banks
of the river.
*(The RUGBY PLAYER puts another cigar in his mouth, and the FIANCÉE
lights it for him.)*
FIANCÉE: Oh! *(She kisses him.)* What white hot coal, what ivory fire spills
from your teeth! My fiancé had cold teeth; he would kiss me, and his lips
would be covered with tiny withered leaves. Such dry lips. I have cut my
braids because he liked them so much, just as I go barefoot now, because
it pleases you. Isn't that true? Isn't that true?
(The RUGBY PLAYER kisses her.)
FIANCÉE: We must leave at once. My fiancé will be here soon.
VOICE: *(At the door.)* Miss!
FIANCÉE: *(Kissing him.)* Go now!
VOICE: Miss!
FIANCÉE: *(Breaking away from the RUGBY PLAYER and affecting a dis-
tracted air.)* I'm coming! *(Softly, to him.)* Good-bye!
*(The RUGBY PLAYER comes back from the balcony and kisses her, lifting
her in his arms.)*
VOICE: Open up!
FIANCÉE: *(Disguising her voice.)* Such little patience!
(The RUGBY PLAYER exits through the balcony, whistling.)
MAID: *(Entering.)* Oh, Miss!
FIANCÉE: Which Miss?
MAID: Miss!
FIANCÉE: What?
*(The ceiling light comes on. It is a bluer light than the one that comes
through the balconies.)*
MAID: Your fiancé has arrived!
FIANCÉE: Fine. Why do you have to get like that?
MAID: *(Tearfully.)* No reason.
FIANCÉE: Where is he?
MAID: Downstairs.
FIANCÉE: With whom?
MAID: With your father.
FIANCÉE: No one else?
MAID: And a gentleman with gold-rimmed spectacles. They were arguing a
great deal.

FIANCÉE: I'm going to get dressed.

(The FIANCÉE sits before the dressing table, and begins to ready herself. The MAID helps her.)

MAID: *(Tearfully.)* Oh, Miss!

FIANCÉE: *(Irritated.)* Which Miss?

MAID: Miss!

FIANCÉE: *(Sourly.)* What?

MAID: Your fiancé is very handsome.

FIANCÉE: Then marry him.

MAID: He's so happy.

FIANCÉE: Yes?

MAID: He brought you this bunch of flowers.

FIANCÉE: You know perfectly well I do not like flowers. Throw them off the balcony.

MAID: But they're so beautiful...! And they've just been cut.

FIANCÉE: *(With authority.)* Throw them out!

(The MAID throws some flowers, which are in a nearby vase, off the balcony.)

MAID: Oh, Miss!

FIANCÉE: *(Furiously.)* Which Miss?

MAID: Miss!

FIANCÉE: Whaaat...!

MAID: Think well what you do. Think on it. The world is big. But we are small.

FIANCÉE: What do you know?

MAID: Yes. Yes, I know. My father was in Brazil twice, and he became so small he could fit inside a suitcase. Things are forgotten, but what's bad remains.

FIANCÉE: I told you to be quiet!

MAID: Oh, Miss!

FIANCÉE: *(Vigorously.)* My clothes!

MAID: What are you going to do?

FIANCÉE: What I can!

MAID: He's such a good man! And he has waited for you for so long. With such hope. Five years. Five years. *(Hands FIANCÉE her clothes.)*

FIANCÉE: Did he shake your hand?

MAID: *(Joyfully.)* Yes. He shook my hand.

FIANCÉE: And how did he shake your hand?

MAID: Very gently, barely squeezing it at all.

FIANCÉE: You see? He did not squeeze you.

MAID: I once had a fiancé who was a soldier, and he would crush the rings against my fingers until I bled. That's why I asked him to leave me.

FIANCÉE: Really?

MAID: Oh, Miss!

FIANCÉE: Which dress shall I wear?

MAID: The red one makes you look lovely.

FIANCÉE: I don't want to look pretty.

MAID: The green one.

FIANCÉE: No.

MAID: The orange?

FIANCÉE: *(Emphatically.)* No.

MAID: The one with the crinoline.

FIANCÉE: *(Even more emphatically.)* No.

MAID: The dress with the autumn leaves?

FIANCÉE: *(Irritated, forcefully.)* I said no. I want to wear an earth-colored habit for this man: a habit of bare rock with a plain belt of hemp around my waist.

(The car horn is heard. The FIANCÉE half-closes her eyes, and with a changed expression, continues to speak.)

FIANCÉE: But with a jasmine collar around my neck, and my whole body wrapped tightly in a veil, still wet from the sea. *(She looks toward the balcony.)*

MAID: Your fiancé better not find out!

FIANCÉE: He'll find out sooner or later. *(Choosing a simple sack dress.)* This one. *(She slips it on.)*

MAID: You're wrong!

FIANCÉE: Why?

MAID: Your fiancé is looking for something else. In my village, there was a young man who used to climb up into the church tower so he could get a closer look at the moon, and his fiancée broke off their engagement.

FIANCÉE: She was right!

MAID: He said he could see his fiancée's face in the moon.

FIANCÉE: *(Emphatically.)* And you think that was true?

(The FIANCÉE finishes fixing herself up at the dressing table, and turns on the angel lamps.)

MAID: When I broke up with the valet…

FIANCÉE: You already broke up with the valet? So handsome…! So handsome…! So handsome…!

MAID: I had to. I gave him a handkerchief that I had embroidered for him with the words "Love, Love, Love," and he lost it.

FIANCÉE: Leave now.

MAID: Should I close the balconies?

FIANCÉE: No.

MAID: The breeze will burn your skin.

FIANCÉE: I would like it to. I want to turn black, darker than any young man. And if I fall, to not bleed; and if I pick a blackberry, to not be pricked by it. Everyone is walking on a tightrope with their eyes closed. I want my feet to be leaden, so that they will always be firm on the ground. Last night I dreamt that all children grow up merely by chance…the power of one kiss could kill them all. A dagger, a pair of scissors lasts forever, and this breast of mine lasts only for a moment in time.

MAID: *(Listening.)* Your father comes.

FIANCÉE: Put all my brightly colored dresses in a suitcase.

MAID: *(Trembling.)* Yes.

FIANCÉE: And have the key to the garage ready.

MAID: *(Fearfully.)* All right!

(The Fiancée's FATHER enters. He is a distracted gentleman. A pair of binoculars hangs from his neck. White wig. Rosy face. He wears a black suit and white gloves. He is extremely short-sighted.)

FATHER: Are you ready?

FIANCÉE: *(Irritated.)* What do I have to be ready for?

FATHER: He has arrived!

FIANCÉE: So?

FATHER: Well, since you are engaged, and we are talking about your life and happiness, it is only natural that you be content, and that you have made up your mind.

FIANCÉE: Well, I am not.

FATHER: What?

FIANCÉE: I am not content. Are you?

FATHER: But, daughter… What is this man going to say?

FIANCÉE: He can say whatever he wants!

FATHER: He has come to marry you. You have written to him during these last five years we have been abroad. You have not danced with anyone on the ocean-liners, you have not shown the slightest interest in anyone else. What has brought about this sudden change?

FIANCÉE: I do not want to see him. I need to live. He talks too much.

FATHER: Oh! Why did you not say this before?

FIANCÉE: Because before I did not exist! The earth and sea existed. But I slept sweetly against the cushions on the train.

FATHER: This man will insult me and with good reason. Dear God! Everything was arranged. I had given you a beautiful wedding dress. It is right there, on the mannequin.

FIANCÉE: Don't talk to me about it. I don't want to hear it.

FATHER: And I? And I? Do not I have the right to rest? Tonight there will be a lunar eclipse. I will not be able to watch it from the terrace now. Once I have become upset, my blood rises and goes straight to my eyes, and I cannot see. What will we do with this man?

FIANCÉE: Whatever you want. I don't want to see him.

FATHER: (*Emphatically, finding the will to go on.*) You must carry on with your engagement!

FIANCÉE: I will not.

FATHER: You must.

FIANCÉE: No.

FATHER: Everyone is against me. (*Looks up at the sky through the balcony.*) Now the eclipse will begin. (*Goes to balcony.*) They have put out all the lights. (*With anguish.*) It will be beautiful! I have been waiting for this for a long time. And now I cannot see it. Why have you deceived him?

FIANCÉE: I have not deceived him.

FATHER: Day by day. For five years. Dear God!

(*The MAID enters suddenly and runs to the balcony. From Off, loud voices can be heard.*)

MAID: They're arguing!

FATHER: Who?

MAID: He's come in. (*She exits quickly.*)

FATHER: What is happening?

FIANCÉE: Where are you going? (*With anguish.*) Close the door.

FATHER: But why?

FIANCÉE: Ah!

(*The YOUNG MAN appears. He wears street clothes. He smoothes his hair. Upon his entrance, all stage lights fade up, as well as the branches of bulbs the angels holds in their hands. FIANCÉE, YOUNG MAN, and FATHER look at one another, still, in silence.*)

YOUNG MAN: Excuse me.

(*Pause.*)

FATHER: (*Embarrassed.*) Sit down.

(The MAID enters nervously with her hands at her breast.)

YOUNG MAN: *(Taking the FIANCÉE's hand.)* It has been such a long trip…

FIANCÉE: *(Fixing her gaze upon him, without letting go of his hand.)* Yes. A cold trip. It has snowed a great deal these last few years. *(She lets go of his hand.)*

YOUNG MAN: You must forgive me, what with all the running and climbing up the stairs, I am a bit unsettled. And then… on the street, I beat some children who were trying to stone a cat to death.

(FATHER offers him a chair.)

FIANCÉE: *(To the MAID.)* A cold hand. A hand of cut wax.

MAID: He will hear you!

FIANCÉE: And an ancient gaze. A gaze that splits in two like the wings of a dried butterfly.

YOUNG MAN: No. I cannot sit. I prefer to talk. Suddenly, while I was climbing up the stairs, all the songs that I had forgotten came to my mind, and I wanted to sing them all at once. *(He draws close to the FIANCÉE.)* Your braids…

FIANCÉE: I have never had braids.

YOUNG MAN: Then it must have been the moonlight. It must have been the air filling its mouth to kiss your head.

(The MAID withdraws to one corner. The FATHER goes to the balcony, and looks out through his binoculars.)

FIANCÉE: Weren't you taller?

YOUNG MAN: No. No.

FIANCÉE: And didn't you have a violent smile that was like a heron's claw on your face?

YOUNG MAN: No.

FIANCÉE: And didn't you play rugby?

YOUNG MAN: Never.

FIANCÉE: *(Passionately.)* And didn't you grab a horse by its mane and kill three thousand pheasants in one day?

YOUNG MAN: Never.

FIANCÉE: Then… why do you come here for me? My hands were full of rings. Where is there a drop of blood?

YOUNG MAN: I will bleed, if it pleases you.

FIANCÉE: *(Vigorously.)* It is not your blood I desire, it is mine!

YOUNG MAN: Now, no one will be able to unwrap my arms from around your neck.

FIANCÉE: They are not your arms, but mine! I am the one who wants to burn in another fire!

YOUNG MAN: There is no other fire but mine. *(He embraces her.)* Because I have waited for you, and now I am rewarded with my dream. And your braids are not a dream because I will weave them with your hair. Nor is your waist a dream because it sings of my blood. It is mine, this blood. I have waited slowly through a long rain, and this dream is mine.

FIANCÉE: *(Disengaging herself from him.)* Leave me. You could have said anything, but the word *dream*. Nobody dreams here. I do not want to dream…

YOUNG MAN: But you love!

FIANCÉE: There is no love here. Go away!

YOUNG MAN: *(Startled.)* What do you say?

FIANCÉE: Look for some other woman's hair to braid.

YOUNG MAN: *(As if waking.)* No.

FIANCÉE: How can I let you come into my bedroom when I have already let someone else in?

YOUNG MAN: *(Covers his face with his hands.)* Oh!

FIANCÉE: Two days, and I already feel weighed down with chains. In the mirrors, in the bed's lace, I already hear a child's cry haunting me.

YOUNG MAN: But my house is already built. I have touched the walls myself. Who is going to live in it now? The wind?

FIANCÉE: Is that my fault? Do you want me to go with you?

YOUNG MAN: *(Sits in chair, dejected.)* Yes, yes, come.

FIANCÉE: A mirror, a table would be closer to you than I could ever be.

YOUNG MAN: What am I going to do now?

FIANCÉE: Love.

YOUNG MAN: Who?

FIANCÉE: Look for someone. In the streets, in the fields…

YOUNG MAN: *(Vigorously.)* I will not look for anyone. I have you. You are here, in my hands, in this moment in time, and you cannot close the door on me, because I come to you wet from a five-year rain. And because there is nothing after this, because I will not be able to love, because all will be over.

FIANCÉE: Let go of me!

YOUNG MAN: What hurts me is not your deceit. You are not altogether bad. You are insignificant. It is my lost treasure. It is my love without purpose. But you will come!

FIANCÉE: I will not!

YOUNG MAN: So that I will not have to begin again. I feel as if I am even forgetting how to speak…

FIANCÉE: I will not go.

YOUNG MAN: So that I will not die. You hear me? So that I will not die.

FIANCÉE: Leave me!

MAID: *(Entering.)* Miss! Sir!

(The YOUNG MAN releases the FIANCÉE.)

FATHER: *(Entering.)* Who is shouting?

FIANCÉE: No one.

FATHER: *(Looking at YOUNG MAN.)* My dear man…

YOUNG MAN: *(Dejected.)* We were talking…

FIANCÉE: *(To FATHER.)* You must return his gifts… *(The YOUNG MAN makes a gesture.)* All of them. It would be unjust… All except for the fans, because they are broken.

YOUNG MAN: *(Remembering.)* Two fans.

FIANCÉE: A blue one…

YOUNG MAN: With three sunken gondolas…

FIANCÉE: And a white one.

YOUNG MAN: Which had a tiger's face in its heart. And… they're broken?

MAID: The coal-man's boy took the last sticks.

FATHER: They were good fans, but we'll…

YOUNG MAN: *(Smiling.)* It doesn't matter that they're lost. I can feel their air burn my skin right now.

MAID: *(To FIANCÉE.)* And the wedding dress, too?

FIANCÉE: Of course.

MAID: *(Tearfully.)* There it is. On the mannequin.

FATHER: *(To YOUNG MAN.)* I wish I could…

YOUNG MAN: It's no matter.

FATHER: In any case, you should make yourself at home.

YOUNG MAN: Thank you!

FATHER: *(Looking toward the balcony.)* It should be starting now. Excuse me. *(To FIANCÉE.)* Are you coming?

FIANCÉE: Yes. *(To YOUNG MAN.)* Good-bye!

YOUNG MAN: Good-bye! *(They exit.)*

VOICE: Good-bye!

YOUNG MAN: Good-bye… what now? What do I do now with this hour that comes upon me, this hour which I do not know? Where do I go? *(Lights dim. The bulbs of the angels' hands give off a blue light. Moonlight begins to seep through the balconies; it increases in intensity until the end of the act. A cry is heard.)*

YOUNG MAN: *(Looks toward the door.)* Who's there?

(The MANNEQUIN enters wearing the wedding dress. This character has a gray face, and eyebrows and lips of gold, like a mannequin in a fancy shop window.)

MANNEQUIN: Who will use the fine silver
of the little dark-haired bride?
My train is swallowed by the sea
and the moon wears my orange-blossom crown.
My ring, sir, my ring of ancient gold,
has sunk in the sands of the mirror.
Who will wear my dress? Who will wear it now?
The river's mouth will wear it to marry the sea.

YOUNG MAN: What do you sing? Tell me.

MANNEQUIN: I sing
of a death I never suffered,
The pain of a useless veil,
a cry of silk and down.
A bodice that will remain
frozen in the dark snow,
where its laces will not be able to
compete with the beauty of the sea-foam.
The cloth that covers the flesh
will ache for warm water.
But instead of a burning touch,
there will be only a broken torso of rain.
Who will wear the fine clothes
of the little dark-haired bride?

YOUNG MAN: The dark wind will put them on
playing at dawn in the grotto,
satin garters for the reeds,
silk stockings for the moon.
Give the white veil to the spiders
so they may eat and cover
the doves, and so become entangled
in its threads of beauty.
No one will wear your dress,
white shape and blurred light,

for silk and frost
are fragile architectures.

MANNEQUIN: My train is swallowed by the sea.

YOUNG MAN: And the moon lifts your orange-blossom crown
Into the air.

MANNEQUIN: *(Annoyed.)* I don't want it to. My silks carry
thread by thread, and one by one,
the heat of a mouth's longing.
And my gown asks
where are the warm hands
that will squeeze its waist?

YOUNG MAN: I also ask. Quiet.

MANNEQUIN: You lie. You're to blame,
colt of lead and foam,
the air broken in your bit,
and the sea tied to your hipbone.
You could have whinnied
but instead you became a sleepy lagoon,
full of dry leaves and moss
where this dress will rot.
My ring, sir, my ring of ancient gold.

YOUNG MAN: Has sunken through the sands in the mirror.

MANNEQUIN: Why didn't you come before?
She waited for you
naked like a wind serpent
fainting on her pillow.

YOUNG MAN: *(Rising.)* Silence! Leave me now! Go away,
or I will break in my rage
the rose-stained monogram
which your white silk hides.
Go to the street to seek
the virgin shoulders of night,
or the six long songs
the guitars will cry.
No one will put on your dress.

MANNEQUIN: I will always follow you.

YOUNG MAN: Never.

MANNEQUIN: Let me talk to you.

YOUNG MAN: It's useless. I don't want to know.

MANNEQUIN: Listen. Look.

YOUNG MAN: What?

MANNEQUIN: A little suit I stole from the sewing room.
   (Holds up a child's pink suit.)

MANNEQUIN: The fountains of wet milk
   soak my threads of anguish
   and a bee's white pain
   covers my nape with rays.
   My son! I want to have my son!
   These ribbons draw his shape
   on my skirt making my waist
   explode with happiness.
   He is your son!

YOUNG MAN: Yes, my son:
   Where the birds of mad dreams and wise jasmine
   come together.
   (Anguished.) And if my son does not come?
   A bird that flies through the air
   cannot sing.

MANNEQUIN: He cannot.

YOUNG MAN: And if my son does not come?
   Boat that plies the seas
   cannot swim.

MANNEQUIN: It cannot.

YOUNG MAN: The rain's harp is still,
   an ocean turned to rock
   laughs its last dark waves.

MANNEQUIN: Who will wear my dress? Who will wear it?

YOUNG MAN: *(With enthusiasm.)* The woman who waits by the seashore
   will put it on.

MANNEQUIN: She will always wait for you, remember?
   She was hidden in your house.
   She loved you and left.
   Your son sings in his cradle
   and since he is a child of snow
   he waits for your blood.
   Run, look for her, quickly!
   And bring her to me naked
   so that my silks may,

thread by thread, and one by one,

open the rose that is hidden

in the flesh of her blond belly.

YOUNG MAN: I must live!

MANNEQUIN: Do not wait!

YOUNG MAN: My child sings in his cradle,

and since he is a child of snow,

he needs my heart, he needs my help.

MANNEQUIN: *(Indicating child's suit.)* Give me the suit.

YOUNG MAN: *(Sweetly.)* No.

MANNEQUIN: *(Tearing it from him.)* I want it.

While you seek and conquer, I will sing a song over your newborn wrinkles.

(Kisses him.)

YOUNG MAN: Right now! Where is she?

MANNEQUIN: On the street.

YOUNG MAN: Before the red moon

washes the perfection of its curves

in the blood of the eclipse,

I will bring my own woman

naked, and trembling with love…

(The light is intensely blue. The MAID enters from stage left with a candelabra, and slowly the lights return to their normal intensity, but without losing the blue light that comes in through the open balconies in the background. As soon as the MAID enters, the MANNEQUIN becomes fixed in a store-window pose, her head inclined, and her hands delicately raised. The MAID leaves the candelabra on the dressing table, looking at the YOUNG MAN all the while with a remorseful attitude. The OLD MAN appears instantly from a door, stage right. The lights grow stronger.)

YOUNG MAN: *(Surprised.)* You.

OLD MAN: *(Agitated, putting his hands to his chest. He has a silk handkerchief in hand.)* Yes. It is I.

(The MAID exits quickly.)

YOUNG MAN: *(Sourly.)* I do not need you.

OLD MAN: Now more than ever. Oh, you have wounded me! Why did you come up the stairs? I knew what was going to happen. Oh…!

YOUNG MAN: *(Sweetly.)* What's wrong?

OLD MAN: *(Vigorously.)* Nothing. Nothing's wrong. I am wounded, but…

the blood dries, and what's past is past. *(The YOUNG MAN begins to exit.)* Where are you going?

YOUNG MAN: *(Joyfully.)* To look.

OLD MAN: For whom?

YOUNG MAN: For the woman who loves me. You saw her in my house, don't you remember?

OLD MAN: I don't remember. Wait.

YOUNG MAN: No. Right now.

(The OLD MAN grabs him by the arm.)

FATHER: *(Entering.)* Daughter! Where are you? Daughter!

(The honking of a car horn is heard.)

MAID: *(On the balcony.)* Miss! Miss!

FATHER: *(Going to the balcony.)* Daughter! Wait, wait! *(Exits.)*

YOUNG MAN: I, too, will go. I, too, will look, as she does, for the new flower of my desire. *(Exits running.)*

OLD MAN: Wait! Wait! Don't leave me wounded like this! Wait! Wait!

(Exits. Voices grow faint.)

MAID: *(Enters quickly, grabs the candelabra and exits through the balcony.)* Oh, Miss. Dear God. Miss!

(Car horn in the distance.)

MANNEQUIN: My ring, sir, my ring of ancient gold.

(Pause.)

MANNEQUIN: Has sunken in the sands of the mirror.

Who will wear my dress? Who will wear it now?

(Pause. She sobs.)

MANNEQUIN: The river's mouth will wear it to marry the sea.

(She faints, and falls upon the sofa.)

VOICE: *(From Off.)* Waaaait...!

(FAST CURTAIN.)

END OF ACT TWO

ACT THREE
SCENE ONE

Forest. Large tree trunks. At center, a theater surrounded by baroque cur-
tains, drawn closed. A small staircase joins the smaller stage to the larger one.
As the main curtain rises, two figures dressed in black cross among the tree
trunks. They have plaster-white faces and white hands. Music is heard in the
distance. The HARLEQUIN appears, dressed in black and green. He carries
two masks, one in each hand. He hides the masks behind his back. He moves
rhythmically, like a dancer.

HARLEQUIN: A dream travels over time
　　floating like a boat on the sea.
　　No one can force open the seeds
　　inside the heart of a dream.
　　(He puts on a mask with a joyful face.)
HARLEQUIN: Oh, how the dawn sings, how it sings!
　　What blue icebergs it brings!
　　(Takes off mask.)
HARLEQUIN: Time travels over a dream,
　　sinking up to its hairs.
　　Today and yesterday eat
　　the dark blossoms of despair.
　　(He puts on a mask with a sleepy expression.)
HARLEQUIN: Oh, how the night sings, how it sings!
　　What a rain of anemones it brings!
　　(He takes off the mask.)
HARLEQUIN: Over the same pillar
　　dream and time are entwined,
　　as is the wail of the child
　　with the broken tongue of the old man.
　　(With one mask.)
HARLEQUIN: Oh, how the dawn sings, how it sings!
　　(With the other.)
HARLEQUIN: What a rain of anemones it brings!
　　And if a dream feigns walls
　　Over the plains of time,
　　Time makes a dream believe
　　it is born at the moment the clock strikes.

Oh, how the night sings, how it sings!
What blue icebergs it brings!
*(From now on, distant mournful hunting horns will be heard in the back-
ground at measured intervals throughout the rest of the act. A GIRL dressed
in a black Greek tunic appears. She jumps, carrying a garland.)*
GIRL: Who believes it?
   Who would believe?
   My lover waits for me
   At the bottom of the sea.
HARLEQUIN: *(Teasing.)* A lie.
GIRL: It's true.
   I lost my thimble,
   I lost my desire,
   And I found them again
   in the trunks of the trees.
HARLEQUIN: *(Ironically.)* A very long rope,
   long enough to take you down.
GIRL: To sharks and fish
   and coral reefs.
HARLEQUIN: Way down.
GIRL: Way down deep.
HARLEQUIN: Asleep.
GIRL: Way down.
   Flags of green water
   name him their chief.
HARLEQUIN: *(Loudly, teasing.)* A lie.
GIRL: *(Loudly.)* It's true.
   I lost my thimble,
   I lost my crown,
   and I found them again
   as I turned halfway around.
HARLEQUIN: Right now.
GIRL: Now?
HARLEQUIN: You will see your lover
   as the wind and sea
   turn halfway around.
GIRL: *(Frightened.)* A lie.
HARLEQUIN: It's true.
   I will give him to you.

GIRL: (*Restless.*) You will not give him to me.
     One can never get to
     the bottom of the sea.
HARLEQUIN: (*Shouting, as if he was in the circus.*) Good man, appear!
     (*A splendid CLOWN appears, full of sequins. His powdered head gives the
     impression of a skull. He laughs loudly and heartily.*)
HARLEQUIN: You will bring
     this girl's
     lover from the sea.
CLOWN: (*Rolls up his sleeves.*) A ladder, please.
GIRL: (*Frightened.*) Yes?
CLOWN: (*To GIRL.*) To go down.
     (*To audience.*)
CLOWN: Good evening!
HARLEQUIN: Bravo!
CLOWN: (*To HARLEQUIN.*) You, look over there!
     (*HARLEQUIN laughs, turns around.*)
CLOWN: Come on, play!
     (*Claps his hands.*)
HARLEQUIN: I play.
     Fiancé, where can you be?
     (*The HARLEQUIN plays on a white violin with two golden strings. It
     should be large and flat. He keeps the tempo with his head.*)
HARLEQUIN: (*Disguising his voice.*) Through the cool seaweed
     I will hunt for
     large sea snails
     and salt lilies.
GIRL: (*Truly frightened.*) I don't want you to.
CLOWN: Silence.
     (*HARLEQUIN laughs.*)
GIRL: (*To CLOWN, with fear.*) I am going to jump
     over the tall grass.
     Later we will go
     to the waters of the sea.
HARLEQUIN: (*Teasing.*) A lie.
GIRL: (*To CLOWN.*) It's true.
     (*She begins to exit, crying.*)
GIRL: Who believes it?
     Who would believe?

I lost my thimble,
I lost my crown.
HARLEQUIN: *(Melancholic.)* As the wind and the sea
turned halfway around.
(The GIRL exits.)
CLOWN: *(Indicating.)* There.
HARLEQUIN: Where? What for?
CLOWN: To perform:
A small boy
who wants to turn
his slivers of bread
into flowers of steel.
HARLEQUIN: A lie.
CLOWN: *(Severely.)* It's true.
I lost my curve and rose,
I lost my necklace
and I found them again
among the freshwater pearls.
HARLEQUIN: *(Adopting a circus pose, as if the boy could hear him.)* Good
man, come here.
(He begins to exit.)
CLOWN: *(Shouting and looking toward the forest, getting ahead of the HAR-
LEQUIN.)* You don't have to scream.
Good day!
(Softly now.)
Come on!
Play.
HARLEQUIN: Play?
CLOWN: *(Out loud.)* A waltz.
(The HARLEQUIN begins to play. In a soft voice now.)
CLOWN: Hurry.
(Out loud.)
Gentlemen:
I will now show you…
HARLEQUIN: That he found them again
among the freshwater pearls.
CLOWN: I will show you…
(Exits.)

HARLEQUIN: *(Exiting.)* The turning wheel
of the wind and the sea.

(Hunting horns are heard. The TYPIST appears. She wears a tennis dress with a brightly colored beret. Over her dress, a long cape. The first MASK accompanies her. The MASK wears a turn-of-the-century dress with a long wild yellow train. Her hair is of yellow silk that falls down her back like a mantle. Her face is a white-plaster mask, and she wears elbow-length white gloves. She also wears a yellow hat, and her breast is covered with gold sequins. The effect of this character should be that of a flame against a background of lunar blue and nocturnal tree trunks. She speaks with a light Italian accent.)

MASK: *(Laughing.)* A true pleasure.

TYPIST: I left the gentlemen's house. I remember that there was a great summer storm the day I left, and that the porter's son had just died. I passed through the library, and he said "Did you call me?" To which I replied, closing my eyes, "No." And later, when I was at the door, he said "Do you need me?" And I said "No, I do not need you."

MASK: Lovely!

TYPIST: He would wait up all night until I appeared at the window.

MASK: And you, signorina typist?

TYPIST: I would not appear. But…I would see him through the cracks…so still *(Takes out handkerchief.)* and with such sad eyes…The air cut through me like a knife, but I couldn't speak to him.

MASK: But why, Miss?

TYPIST: Because he loved me too much.

MASK: Oh mio Dio! It was the same with my Count Arturo of Italy. Oh love!

TYPIST: Really?

MASK: In the foyer of the Paris Opera, there are enormous balustrades that open out onto the sea. Count Arturo, with a camellia between his teeth, would pass by in a small boat with his child. I had abandoned them both, you see. But I simply closed the curtains and tossed them a diamond. Oh, what sweet torment, my friend! *(Weeps.)* The count and his boy went hungry and slept among the branches with a greyhound that a Russian gentlemen had given me. *(Vigorously pleading.)* Can you spare a tiny crust of bread for me? Can you spare a tiny crust of bread for my son? For the boy Count Arturo left to die in the frost?…*(Agitated.)* And later I went to the hospital and it was there that I learned that the count had married a great Roman lady… Since then, I have lived by begging, and sharing my bed with the men who unload the coal at the docks.

TYPIST: What are you saying? Why do you talk like this?

MASK: *(Calming herself.)* I only say that Count Arturo loved me so much that he cried behind the curtains with his child, while I was like a silver half moon through the binoculars and the gaslight that glimmered beneath the dome of the Grande Opera of Paris.

TYPIST: Delicious. And when does the count arrive?

MASK: And when does your friend arrive?

TYPIST: He will be late.

MASK: So will Arturo. He has a scar on his right hand where he has cut with a dagger…over me, of course. *(Holding out her hand.)* See? *(Pointing to her neck.)* And here another, see?

TYPIST: Yes, but why?

MASK: Why? Why? Why shouldn't I have wounds? Who carries the wounds of my count?

TYPIST: You do. It's true! He has been waiting for me for five years, and yet… How beautiful it is to wait with the certainty that the time will come when you will be loved.

MASK: And it is certain!

TYPIST: Certainly! That's why we should laugh! When I was small, I used to save the sweets so I could eat them later.

MASK: Ha, ha, ha! Yes, it's true. They taste better that way.

(Hunting horns are heard.)

TYPIST: *(Starts to exit.)* If my friend should come—so tall, with his hair full of curls, but curled in a special way—please act like you don't know him.

MASK: Of course, my friend. *(Gathers her train.)*

(The YOUNG MAN appears. He wears gray knickers with blue-checked socks.)

HARLEQUIN: *(Entering.)* Hey!

YOUNG MAN: What?

HARLEQUIN: Where are you going?

YOUNG MAN: Home.

HARLEQUIN: *(Ironically.)* Is that so?

YOUNG MAN: Naturally. *(Starts to walk away.)*

HARLEQUIN: Hey! You can't go through there.

YOUNG MAN: Has the road been closed?

HARLEQUIN: The circus is over there.

YOUNG MAN: Very well. *(Turns around.)*

HARLEQUIN: Full of spectators who are terribly still. *(Softly.)* Wouldn't the gentlemen like to go in?

YOUNG MAN: No.

HARLEQUIN: *(Emphatically.)* Virgil, the poet, made a fly out of gold, and all the flies that poisoned the air of Naples died. Over there, in the circus, there is enough soft gold to make a statue the same size as...yourself.

YOUNG MAN: Is Poplar Street also blocked?

HARLEQUIN: The wagons and the cages for the serpents are there.

YOUNG MAN: Then I will go back the way I came. *(Starts to exit.)*

CLOWN: *(Entering from the opposite side.)* Where are you going? Ha, ha, ha.

HARLEQUIN: He says he's going home.

CLOWN: *(Gives the HARLEQUIN a circus slap.)* Take this home!

HARLEQUIN: *(Falls to the ground, shouting.)* Oh, it hurts, it hurts!

CLOWN: *(To YOUNG MAN.)* Come here!

YOUNG MAN: *(Annoyed.)* You want to tell me what kind of joke this is? I was on my way home. That is to say, not my house, someone else's house, to...

CLOWN: *(Interrupting.)* To look.

YOUNG MAN: Yes, because I need to look.

CLOWN: *(Cheerfully.)* Look. Turn halfway around and you will find it.

TYPIST'S VOICE: *(Singing.)* Where are you going, my love,
my love,
with the air in a glass
and the sea in a jar?
(The HARLEQUIN rises. The YOUNG MAN has his back turned. The CLOWN and HARLEQUIN exit without turning their backs to him, on tiptoe, with a dance step, and their fingers to their lips.)

YOUNG MAN: *(Astonished.)* Where are you going, my love,
my life, my love,
with the air in a glass
and the sea in a jar?

TYPIST: *(Appearing.)* Where? Wherever I am called.

YOUNG MAN: My life!

TYPIST: With you alone.

YOUNG MAN: I am to bring your naked, immaculate body,
wrinkled like a rose,
to the place where the silkworms
tremble with cold.
White sheets await you.
Come quickly now. Let's go.

Before the yellow nightingales
In the trees begin to moan.
TYPIST: Yes. The sun is a hawk.
Better yet: a falcon of glass.
No: The sun is a large tree trunk,
and you are the river's shadow.
Tell me, if you were to embrace me,
would not the reeds and lilies be born,
would not your arms discolor my clothes?
Love, leave me on the mount
filled with the clouds and the dew,
so I can watch your great sadness,
envelop the sleeping sky.
YOUNG MAN: Do not say such things, child. Let's go.
I do not want to lose any more time.
A pure blood and a deep fever
take me now to some other place.
I want to live.
TYPIST: With whom?
YOUNG MAN: With you.
TYPIST: What is that sound I hear in the distance?
YOUNG MAN: Love,
It is the day that returns.
My love!
TYPIST: *(Content, as if in a dream.)* A nightingale that sings,
an afternoon's gray nightingale
on the air's wing.
Nightingale, I have heard you.
I want to live.
YOUNG MAN: With whom?
TYPIST: With the river's shadow.
(In anguish and hiding her head in the YOUNG MAN's chest, she cries.)
TYPIST: What is that sound I hear in the distance?
YOUNG MAN: Love,
it is the blood inside my throat,
my love.
TYPIST: It will always be like this. Always.
Whether we are asleep or awake.

YOUNG MAN: Never like this. Never, never!

Let us leave this place. Go.

TYPIST: Wait!

YOUNG MAN: Love does not wait!

TYPIST: *(Disengaging herself from the YOUNG MAN.)* Where are you going, my love,

with the air in a glass,

and the sea in a jar?

(The TYPIST heads toward the staircase. The curtains of the small theater are drawn, and the library from the first act is revealed, smaller and in paler hues. The yellow MASK appears on the small stage. She has a lace handkerchief in her hand, and constantly sniffs from a bottle of smelling salts.)

MASK: I have just left the count forever. He's back there with his boy. *(Descends the stairs.)* I am sure he will die. He loved me so much, so much. *(Weeps. To the TYPIST.)* Didn't you know? His child is going to die in the frost. I have abandoned him. Don't you see how happy I am? Don't you see how I laugh? *(Weeps.)* Now he will look for me everywhere. *(Throws herself on the ground.)* I am going to hide behind the blackberry bush, *(Softly.)* behind the blackberries. I only talk like this because I do not want Arturo to hear me. *(Out loud.)* I do not want to! I have already told you I do not love you! *(Exits crying.)* You love me. Yes. But I? I do not love you.

(Two SERVANTS appear dressed in blue livery with very pale faces. They place two white stools stage left. The SERVANT from the first act crosses the small stage, always on tiptoe.)

TYPIST: *(To the SERVANT while climbing the stairs to the small stage.)* If a gentleman arrives, let him come in. *(On the small stage.)* Although he won't come until he is due.

(The YOUNG MAN starts to slowly ascend the stairs.)

YOUNG MAN: *(On the small stage, passionately.)* Are you happy here?

TYPIST: Have you written the letters?

YOUNG MAN: It's nicer upstairs. Come!

TYPIST: I have loved you so much!

YOUNG MAN: I love you so much!

TYPIST: I will love you so much!

YOUNG MAN: I would die without you. Where would I go if you leave me? I do not remember anything. The other one doesn't exist. But you do, because you love me.

TYPIST: I have loved you, dear! I will love you always.

YOUNG MAN: Now…

TYPIST: What do you mean "now"?

(*The OLD MAN appears. He is dressed in blue and has a large, blood-stained handkerchief in hand. He holds the handkerchief to his face and chest. He seems troubled, and watches carefully all that happens on the small stage.*)

YOUNG MAN: I have waited and died.

TYPIST: I died waiting.

YOUNG MAN: But the blood pounds my temples with its small knots of fire, and now you are here.

VOICE: (*From Off.*) My son! My son!

(*The dead BOY crosses the small stage, alone, and goes through a door, stage left.*)

YOUNG MAN: Yes, my son. He runs inside of me like a little ant alone in a closed box. (*To TYPIST.*) A bit of light for my son. Please. He is so small… He presses his little nose against the windows of my heart, and yet, has no air.

(*The yellow MASK appears on the main stage.*)

MASK: My son!

(*TWO MASKS enter, and witness the scene.*)

TYPIST: (*Dryly, with authority.*) Have you written the letters? It isn't your son. It's me. You have waited, and by doing so, you have let me go away, but you have always suspected, my love. Do I lie?

YOUNG MAN: (*Impatiently.*) No, but…

TYPIST: I, in turn, knew you would never love me. And yet, I have raised up my love and I have changed you. I have seen you in the corners of my house. (*Passionately.*) I love you, but only from a distance. I have run so far that I need to look at the sea to be able to recall your trembling lips.

OLD MAN: Because if he is twenty, he can have twenty moons.

TYPIST: (*Lyrical.*) Twenty roses, twenty snows.

YOUNG MAN: (*Annoyed.*) Quiet. You will come with me because you love me, and because I need to live.

TYPIST: Yes. I love you, but much more than that! You haven't the eyes to see me naked, nor the mouth to kiss my never-ending body. Leave me alone! I love you too much to be able to look at you.

YOUNG MAN: Not a minute more! Let's go! (*Grabs her by the wrists.*)

TYPIST: You're hurting me, my love.

YOUNG MAN: So you can feel me.

TYPIST: (*Sweetly.*) Wait…I will go…always. (*Embraces him.*)

OLD MAN: She will go with you. Sit down, my friend. Wait.

YOUNG MAN: *(Anguished.)* No.

TYPIST: I am so far away from you. Why did you leave me? I was dying of cold, and had to look for your love where there was no one, no one at all. But I will stay with you. Let me come down to you, little by little, until I reach you.

(The CLOWN and HARLEQUIN appear. The CLOWN has a concertina, and the HARLEQUIN has a white violin. They sit on the stools.)

CLOWN: A song.

HARLEQUIN: Of years.

CLOWN: Of seas and moons that have never been opened.

HARLEQUIN: And back there?

CLOWN: A shroud of air.

And the music of the violin.

YOUNG MAN: *(Waking from a dream.)* Let's go.

TYPIST: Yes… Can this possibly be you? All of a sudden, like this, without having to slowly ponder this lovely thought: until tomorrow then? Doesn't it make you feel sorry for me?

YOUNG MAN: There's a kind of nest upstairs. You can hear the nightingale sing…and even if you can't hear it, even if a bat beats on the window…

TYPIST: Yes, yes, but…

YOUNG MAN: *(Forcefully.)* Your mouth! *(He kisses her.)*

TYPIST: Later…

YOUNG MAN: *(Passionately.)* Yes. It's better at night.

TYPIST: I will come.

YOUNG MAN: Without fail!

TYPIST: I want to! Listen.

YOUNG MAN: Come on!

TYPIST: But…

YOUNG MAN: Tell me.

TYPIST: I will come with you!

YOUNG MAN: Love! I will come with you.

TYPIST: *(Timidly.)* As five years pass.

YOUNG MAN: Ah! *(Puts his hand to his forehead.)*

OLD MAN: *(Softly.)* Bravo.

(The YOUNG MAN begins to slowly descend the stairs. The TYPIST remains frozen in ecstasy on the stage. The SERVANT enters on tiptoe and covers her with a large white cape.)

CLOWN: A song.

HARLEQUIN: Of years.

CLOWN: Of seas and moons that have never been opened. And back there?

HARLEQUIN: A shroud of air.

CLOWN: And the music of your violin. *(They play.)*

(The yellow MASK appears.)

MASK: The count kisses the portrait where I am an Amazon.

OLD MAN: We won't get anywhere, but we'll go on.

YOUNG MAN: *(Desperately, to CLOWN.)* The exit. Where is it?

TYPIST: *(On the small stage, as if in a dream.)* Love, love.

YOUNG MAN: *(Shaking.)* Show me the door.

CLOWN: *(Ironically, pointing to the left.)* That way.

HARLEQUIN: *(Pointing to the right.)* That way.

TYPIST: I wait for you, my love! I wait for you! Come back soon!

HARLEQUIN: *(Ironically.)* That way.

YOUNG MAN: *(To CLOWN.)* I will knock over all your tents and cages. I know how to jump over a wall.

OLD MAN: *(Anguished.)* This way.

YOUNG MAN: I want to go back. Let me go!

HARLEQUIN: The wind remains.

CLOWN: And the music of your violin.

(Curtain.)

SCENE TWO

The same library as in the first act. To the left, there is the wedding dress on an armless, headless mannequin. There are several open suitcases about the room. To the right, there is a table. The SERVANT and the MAID enter.

MAID: *(Surprised.)* Yes?

SERVANT: She's a porter's wife now, but she used to be a great lady once. She lived for a long time with a very rich Italian count, the father of the boy they just buried.

MAID: My poor dear! How lovely he looked!

SERVANT: It was then that she acquired her delusions of grandeur. That's why she's spent everything she has on the child's clothes and on his coffin.

MAID: And on the flowers! I gave her a small bunch of roses, but they were so small that they didn't even put them in his room.

YOUNG MAN: *(Entering.)* John.

SERVANT: Sir.

(The MAID exits.)

YOUNG MAN: Give me a glass of cold water. *(He seems desperate and physically exhausted.)*

(The SERVANT serves him.)

YOUNG MAN: Wasn't that window much bigger once?

SERVANT: No.

YOUNG MAN: I can't believe it is so narrow. My house had a huge patio, where I used to play with my ponies. I saw it when I was twenty, and it was so small that it seemed incredible to me that I could have flown around in it so much.

SERVANT: Sir, are you feeling all right?

YOUNG MAN: Does a fountain feel all right spouting water? Answer me.

SERVANT: I don't know.

YOUNG MAN: Does a weathervane feel all right turning wherever the wind wants it to?

SERVANT: Sir, you use such examples... But I would ask you, if you would permit me, sir... is the wind all right?

YOUNG MAN: *(Curtly.)* I feel fine.

SERVANT: Did you get enough rest after your trip?

YOUNGMAN: Yes.

SERVANT: A cause for infinite joy. *(Starts to exit.)*

YOUNG MAN: John, are my clothes ready?

SERVANT: Yes, sir. They are in your bedroom.

YOUNG MAN: Which suit?

SERVANT: Your tails. I have laid them out on your bed.

YOUNG MAN: *(Agitated.)* Well, take them off the bed. I don't want to go up and find them laid out all alone on such a big bed, such an empty bed. I don't know who thought of buying it. I had another one once, a small bed. Remember?

SERVANT: Yes, sir. The one made of carved walnut.

YOUNG MAN: That's the one. The bed of carved walnut. How well I slept on that bed. I remember that as a child an enormous moon was born through the railings of the bed...or was it through the railings of the balcony? I don't know. Where is that bed?

SERVANT: You gave it away, sir.

YOUNG MAN: *(In thought.)* To whom?

SERVANT: *(Solemnly.)* To your former typist.

(The YOUNG MAN remains lost in thought.)

YOUNG MAN: *(Indicating to the SERVANT that he may go.)* Very well.
(The SERVANT walks away.)

YOUNG MAN: *(With anguish.)* John!

SERVANT: *(Sternly.)* Sir.

YOUNG MAN: By any chance, did you put out my patent leather shoes?

SERVANT: The pair with the black silk laces.

YOUNG MAN: Black silk… No… Find another pair. *(Rising.)* And is it possible that the air in this house is always heavy? I am going to cut all the flowers in the garden, especially that damn oleander that climbs over the wall, and those weeds that only bloom at midnight.

SERVANT: They say that anemones and poppies can give you a headache at certain hours of the day.

YOUNG MAN: That must be what it is. *(Pointing at dress.)* Take this, too. Put it away in the attic.

SERVANT: Very well. *(About to exit.)*

YOUNG MAN: *(Shyly.)* And leave the patent leather shoes. Just change the laces.
(The doorbell rings.)

SERVANT: *(Entering.)* The young gentlemen are here to play.

YOUNG MAN: *(Annoyed.)* Ah!

SERVANT: *(At the door.)* You will need to get dressed, sir.

YOUNG MAN: *(Exiting.)* Yes. *(Exits almost like a shadow.)*
(The PLAYERS enter. There are three of them. They wear tails, and long capes of white satin that come down to their feet.)

FIRST PLAYER: It was in Venice. A bad year for the game. But that boy played for real. He was pale, so pale that on the last hand, he had no choice but to play the ace of hearts. His own heart, full of blood. He played it, but when I went to take it *(Lowering his voice.)* to… *(looks around.)* he had an ace of cups overflowing to the brim, and he fled drinking from it, with two girls, along the Grand Canal.

SECOND PLAYER: You shouldn't trust the pale ones or the people who are tired of it all. They play, but they hold back.

THIRD PLAYER: I played against this old man in India once. When he didn't have a drop of blood left on the cards, and I was waiting for the right moment to throw myself at him, he stained all the cups red with a special dye and then he escaped through the trees.

FIRST PLAYER: We play and we win, but what a chore it is! The cards drink thick blood from their hands, and it is difficult to cut the thread that joins them.

SECOND PLAYER: But I think with this one… we are not mistaken.

THIRD PLAYER: I don't know.

FIRST PLAYER: *(To SECOND PLAYER.)* You will never learn to know your customers. This one? Life pours out of his pupils, wetting the corner of his lips, and dying his white shirt blue.

SECOND PLAYER: Yes. But remember the child in Switzerland who was nearly dead when he played with us, and almost left all three of us blind with the gush of blood he aimed at us.

THIRD PLAYER: The deck. *(Takes out a deck of cards.)*

SECOND PLAYER: We have to be very gentle with him, so he won't be scared.

THIRD PLAYER: Although I don't think either one of the other, Miss Typist, will think of stopping by here until five years pass, if they show up…

THIRD PLAYER: *(Laughing.)* If they show up. Ha!

FIRST PLAYER: It wouldn't be so bad to play him fast.

SECOND PLAYER: He's holding an ace.

THIRD PLAYER: He has a young heart. Arrows will probably slide right off it.

FIRST PLAYER: *(Brightly, deeply.)* I use arrows in target shooting.

SECOND PLAYER: *(With curiosity.)* Where?

FIRST PLAYER: *(Joking.)* At a target shoot. They stick to the hardest steel as well as the finest gauze, and that's difficult indeed! *(They laugh.)*

SECOND PLAYER: In the end, we shall see.

(The YOUNG MAN appears, wearing tails.)

YOUNG MAN: Gentlemen. *(He shakes their hands.)* You're early. It's awfully hot.

FIRST PLAYER: Not really.

SECOND PLAYER: *(To YOUNG MAN.)* Elegant as always.

FIRST PLAYER: So elegant he need not undress ever again.

THIRD PLAYER: There are times when clothes fit us so well, we do not wish to…

SECOND PLAYER: *(Interrupting.)* That we cannot tear them away from our bodies.

YOUNG MAN: *(Upset.)* You're too kind.

(The SERVANT appears with a tray full of glasses, which he leaves on the table.)

YOUNG MAN: Shall we begin?

(The three PLAYERS sit down.)

FIRST PLAYER: Ready.

SECOND PLAYER: *(Softly.)* Keep your eye on him.

THIRD PLAYER: Won't you sit down?

YOUNG MAN: No… I prefer to stand while I play.

THIRD PLAYER: To stand?

SECOND PLAYER: *(Softly.)* You will need to get in deep.

FIRST PLAYER: *(Dealing cards.)* How many?

YOUNG MAN: Four. *(Cuts for himself and the others.)*

THIRD PLAYER: *(Softly.)* No play.

YOUNG MAN: What cold cards! Nothing. *(Leaves them on the table.)* And you?

FIRST PLAYER: *(Softly.)* Nothing. *(Deals cards again.)*

SECOND PLAYER: *(Looking at cards.)* Nothing. Terrific.

THIRD PLAYER: *(Looks at cards nervously.)* Nothing. We'll see.

FIRST PLAYER: *(To YOUNG MAN.)* Your play.

YOUNG MAN: *(Content.)* And I play. *(Throws one card on the table.)*

FIRST PLAYER: *(Forcefully.)* And I.

SECOND PLAYER: And I.

THIRD PLAYER: And I.

YOUNG MAN: *(Excitedly, with card.)* And now?

> *(The three PLAYERS show their hands. The YOUNG MAN hesitates and hides his hand.)*

YOUNG MAN: John. Serve these gentlemen their liquor.

FIRST PLAYER: *(Gently.)* Would you be so kind as to play your card?

YOUNG MAN: *(Anguished.)* What would you like to drink?

SECOND PLAYER: *(Sweetly.)* The card?

YOUNG MAN: *(To THIRD PLAYER.)* You'll like the anisette. It's a drink that…

THIRD PLAYER: Please…the card…

> *(The SERVANT enters.)*

YOUNG MAN: *(To SERVANT.)* What? Is there no whiskey?

> *(At the very instant the SERVANT enters, the three PLAYERS fall silent with their cards in their hands.)*

YOUNG MAN: Is there no cognac?

FIRST PLAYER: *(Softly, concealing himself from the SERVANT.)* The card.

YOUNG MAN: *(Anguished.)* Cognac is a drink for men who know how to fight.

SECOND PLAYER: *(Softly but forcefully.)* The card.

YOUNG MAN: Or would you prefer chartreuse?

> *(The SERVANT exits.)*

FIRST PLAYER: *(Rising, forcefully.)* Be so kind as to play.

YOUNG MAN: Right now. But first, let us drink.

THIRD PLAYER: *(Powerfully.)* You must play!

YOUNG MAN: *(Agonizing.)* Yes. Yes. A sip of chartreuse. Chartreuse is like a great green-mooned night inside a castle where there is a young man wrapped in golden seaweed.

FIRST PLAYER: *(Powerfully.)* You must give us your ace.

YOUNG MAN: *(Aside.)* My heart.

SECOND PLAYER: *(Emphatically.)* Because you must either win or lose. Come now. Your card.

THIRD PLAYER: Let's go.

FIRST PLAYER: Make your play.

YOUNG MAN: *(Painfully.)* My card.

FIRST PLAYER: The last one.

YOUNG MAN: And I play. *(He places the card on the table.)*

(At this moment, an ace of hearts appears illuminated against the book-shelves of the library. FIRST PLAYER draws a pistol and, without a sound, fires an arrow. The ace of hearts disappears, and the YOUNG MAN puts his hands to his heart.)

FIRST PLAYER: We must leave.

SECOND PLAYER: *(Emphatically.)* We shouldn't wait.

THIRD PLAYER: Cut. Cut carefully.

(The FIRST PLAYER makes a few cuts in the air with a pair of scissors.)

FIRST PLAYER: *(Softly.)* Let's go.

SECOND PLAYER: Quickly. *(They exit.)*

THIRD PLAYER: One must never wait.

YOUNG MAN: John, John. One must live.

ECHO: John, John.

YOUNG MAN: *(Dying.)* I have lost everything.

ECHO: I have lost everything.

YOUNG MAN: My love…

ECHO: Love.

YOUNG MAN: *(On the sofa.)* John.

ECHO: John.

YOUNG MAN: Isn't there…?

ECHO: Isn't there…

SECOND ECHO: *(Very distant.)* Isn't there…?

YOUNG MAN: Anyone here?

ECHO: Here.

SECOND ECHO: Here…

(The YOUNG MAN dies. The SERVANT appears with a lit candelabra. The clock strikes twelve. Curtain.)

END OF PLAY

LORCA CELEBRATION AT INTAR

In celebration of 100 years of Federico García Lorca, INTAR Hispanic-American Art Center organized English performances of Lorca's *The House of Bernarda Alba*, *The Shoemaker's Prodigious Wife*, and *As Five Years Pass* from October 27 to November 29, 1998. The tribute also featured Fernando Arrabal, one of the twentieth-century's foremost Spanish playwrights, who conducted three lectures that explored both the historical and literary context of Lorca's work.

Of the three plays featured, the least known is *As Five Years Pass*. With a minimalist stage set, director Michael John Garces cleverly carved out dream spaces, such as the open window and the portable frame. Characters passed in and out of these locations changing roles, defying time and distance in a surrealist performance. Both the window and the frame marked the threshold to a surrealist world where boundaries between male and female, life and death, past and present are blurred. The area behind the window became a site from which to observe or be observed, as well as a veritable dressing room for the more sublime characters. Momentarily framed by the window of surrealism, those who acrobatically climbed, slithered, or rolled onto the stage, undermined the traditional stage entrance.

The production included impressive doubling on the part of the actors, whose ability to manage several roles further broke down the barrier between the real and the surreal. Marilyn Torres crossed gender and class lines with her stellar performances, that ranged from Tomcat to Maid to Countess. Wearing blue satin pajamas, coupled with her own petite physique and dainty voice, Torres effectively feminized her performance as Tomcat. Mercedes Herrero, dressed to suit her part as the typist, made an otherwise dull role humorous. To her credit, and that of the makeup artist, one of her most charming performances was as the mannequin. Once again her adeptness at humor shone and endeared her to the audience.

Caridad Svich, an acclaimed playwright with a 1992 INTAR production of *Any Place But Here* and a forthcoming anthology of Latino/a plays and performance texts already to her credit, may also add to her merits the fine translation of *As Five Years Pass*. With a dynamic cast, fluent translation, and creative stage sets, the play received great applause. After the November 12th performance the lobby was crowded with people waiting to congratulate the actors. Among those in attendance that evening were playwright Fernando Arrabal, and Miriam Colon Valle, the founder of the Puerto Rican Traveling Theater.

Lissette Camacho, Rutgers University

Yetta Gottesman as Boy and Marilyn Torres as Cat
from *As Five Years Pass*
Intar Theatre, New York, New York, 1998

photo by Sturgis Warner

LOOKING FOR LORCA:
A LEGACY IN THE AMERICAS

By Caridad Svich

Birth of a poet

Cien años.
Hace cien años
Nacio un poeta
Con una corona de rosas
Sobre su cabeza
Y unas espinas aterciopeladas.

El poeta cantaba
En su cuna.
El poeta lloraba.
Y su grito, su canto
Se oyen
Este día de mañana.

Esta mañana de cien años
Desde que nacio
El poeta. [1]

In 1898, a year that would give us George Gershwin and Bertolt Brecht, Federico García Lorca was born in Granada. In 1998, on the centennial of his birth, and sixty-two years after his death, Hispanic playwrights in the Americas celebrated his legacy as they search for his spirit in their work.

Contemporary American-based Hispanic dramatists like Maria Irene Fornes, Migdalia Cruz, and Jose Rivera along with their counterparts in Central and South America have regarded Federico García Lorca's work as the seminal influence and inspiration for the re-visioning of a new theater.

Drawing on Lorca's experimental work, in particular, a new generation of playwrights have sought to extend the vocabulary of dramatic writing, and expand on "Lorcan" fusions of time and space, realism and symbolism, poetry and prose, music and masque. Whether directly acknowledging García Lorca's influence or not, these dramatists have taken elements and ideas from his work and forged a "hybrid" theater that is both Hispanic and American, and that is still very much in the making, thus developing Lorca's "theater for tomorrow" into a theater for today.

ALPHABETICAL LORCA

Alma, grito, duende. Fluid time: past, present, and future. Compressed time: raging against the elements, hurling against walls. Blood, fire, and sand. A theater of elements. A theater of song. Exasperated clowns, wooden swords, and merciless violence. In Lorca, death is always real, resurrection is not possible. A Catholic theater of priests and satyrs, ceremonies and crimes. A theater of images where green walls, white roses, and black wedding gowns appear out of the air and talk to the moon. A theater of women: destroyed, destroying, triumphant, and willful. Where men are complex and weak, virile and mysterious.

An erotic theater that places sexuality at its center, denouncing cruelty, and the contradictions of society's basic institutions. Authority be damned. A theater of nature, hell, and Spain. A theater for the world.

The first time I heard Lorca's name was in my Spanish class in high school in Charlotte, North Carolina. In the United States. My teacher told us there was a poet whose work we should read. His name was García Lorca and he was born in 1898. "Read this," he said as he tossed a slim volume into our eager hands, "and report on it tomorrow." It was a collection of poems entitled *Romancero Gitano.* I looked at this slim book with a mixture of fear and awe. "Oh odd-shaped moon against a silver sky," I thought "what am I to make of you?" They were "ballads," our teacher told us, "songs." Did we know what "cante jondo" was? I had heard bits of flamenco when I was a child. My grandparents were from Spain—Galicia. And, of course, I had seen the Saturday morning cartoons on television, animated figures stomping and clapping and throwing their voices, but no, I did not know deep song, where the throat reaches back into a place unknown and produces a sound that has no name, except for "the blues." Yes, I had heard the blues. And the Gypsy ballads went into me, and ignited something in my brain. "Lorca was a poet," our teacher said, "one of the greats. And a playwright, too." Is it any coincidence that I started writing plays shortly after reading Lorca's work for the first time?

ORIGIN: IMPRINT

From this early contact with García Lorca's work and subsequent personal rediscoveries of his work over time, certain elements began to make themselves manifest in my own writing for the theater: inscriptions on the body, the public vs. the private, the elements vs. human nature, beauty as aesthetic and form, dream as structure, locating the elemental in the strange, and the fantastical in the commonplace, the art of burning yourself through until there is no trace.

With each Lorca play I have translated into English—*The Love of Don Perlimplín for Belisa in the Garden, As Five Years Pass, Chimera, Buster Keaton Takes a Walk,* and *The Maiden, The Sailor, and The Student*—the struggle and responsibility of the translation process illuminate the difficulty of negotiating not only Spanish and English but also the dilemma of how to interact with a mystery over time—how a text can only give you a phantom memory, whereby one is always constantly in the shadows, chasing after Lorca.

VISION

> SELAH: Spirit is vision: Fragment and memory reflected in the mind's eye. You got to see it. Inside you. It's in the heart where we see things. It's in the heart where we lay to rest trouble and joy. [2]

Lorca's ghost came to visit me as I wove together the tapestry of scenes that would become *Alchemy of Desire / Dead-Man's Blues*, which premiered at the Cincinnati Playhouse in Ohio in 1994. After years of writing and exploring different themes in my work, it was Lorca, and the memory of how I felt when I came upon his work for the first time in high school, that made me return to a place in my writing of "deep song," and allowed me to rediscover the joy of creating a text that could incorporate poetry, song, ritual, image, and traditional Western narrative—the kind of text that is still considered "alternative" today in some circles, even though its roots go beyond Lorca to the *autos sacramentales* of medieval Spain and the work of Euripides and the Greeks.

A story about a grieving war widow, and the four neighborhood women who console her, *Alchemy of Desire / Dead-Man's Blues* is "Lorcan" in spirit, owing a small but significant debt to *The House of Bernarda Alba* as well as other works by Lorca. As Maria Delgado has noted in her eloquent introductory essay "From the UK: A European perspective on Latino theater" in the anthology of Latina/o plays and performance texts *Out of the Fringe*, the play *Alchemy of Desire / Dead-Man's Blues* has a "female chorus that evokes [...] the washerwomen of *Yerma* [...] As with the female protagonists of *Blood Wedding*, for the women of the play, the loss of lovers, husbands, and children is a brutal fact of their existence." However, this play does not merely acknowledge its debt to Lorca, it is also part of an emerging body of Hispanic performance literature that is "hybrid" in nature and slowly changing the face of American drama.

That Latino playwrights have drawn blood from Lorca's work to create their own is important to the understanding of a theater whose history is only beginning to be fully documented. Hispanic drama, which encompasses the work of United States–born or –based Latinas and its relationship to the work of their colleagues in Central and South America, as it responds to or diverges from the Iberian dramatic tradition, has taken Lorca at his word, and broken free of mainstream theatrical constraints. However, especially in the United States, this has been achieved without access to stage representations of Lorca's work outside of the primarily academic arena. García Lorca's theater remains unknown to the general public. The major theatrical institutions have, for the most part, neglected to stage his work, refusing to acknowledge his importance as a world theatrical figure. This lack of access to the experience of witnessing Lorca's work in the performance arena has made his influence on American-based Latino/a playwrights a purely literary one. As Lorca's work has been marginalized in the United States, it has also caused writers of Hispanic origin to be marginalized. Thus, it has left Latino/a playwrights looking for Lorca and has made his legacy all the more poignant.

POET IN THE UNITED STATES:
WHERE IS LORCA?

"There's this code of honor that we all seem to be struggling with," playwright José Rivera has noted, "being Latino in the United States is like being caught in the middle between tradition and non-tradition. But we have come to feel comfortable with contradiction."[3] In a country with its own rich indigenous and Spanish colonial history, and an ever-increasing Hispanic population, mainstream culture, and therefore mainstream theater, which encompasses United States regional theater and the mecca of New York, persists in de-valuing the works of the great Spanish dramatists from Calderon de la Barca to Valle-Inclán to Buero Vallejo to García Lorca, and today's adventurous playwrights like Paloma Pedrero and beyond.

If one were to look at a record of any given season over the last ten years, one would be hard pressed to find more than five major productions of García Lorca's work, and by "major" I mean a production by a theater that has considerable impact on its specific regional community and/or the national cultural radar, such as it is. As critic Lindy Zesch has recently observed, "The fact that the U.S. is itself the fourth-largest Spanish-speaking country in the world has had little impact on our theater and festival repertoires. Latin American plays are infrequently translated and produced, [and] theaters from Latin America rarely tour the U.S."[4] The bulk of the presentations of Lorca's work can be found in the university arena, fueled by students and academics eager to test the theatrical concepts posited by Lorca, especially in works like *As Five Years Pass* and *The Public*. The rest of the presentations of his body of theatrical work have been shouldered by the nation's Hispanic theaters like Repertorio Español and Intar in New York, and Bilingual Foundation for the Arts in Los Angeles, companies that are regarded by the press and the larger "official" theatrical community as theaters that exist merely to "serve" the Latino community, as social work "serves." Thus, these brave professional companies, which have spent as much as twenty-five to thirty years building an audience and struggling to solidify their reputation, are marginalized by their very existence.

To a generation of Latina dramatists raised in the United States, García Lorca's isolation has offered a curious kind of solace. His literary example, and this his legend, have made him a banner figure, a totem, representing all those who have been artistically marginalized: queer Lorca, feminist Lorca, Lorca of Spain, the "invisible" European country, Lorca of the strange.

Geography:
New York—Fornes, Cruz, and Rivera

Cuban-born, New York–based dramatist Maria Irene Fornes' substantial body of work has made her a pioneer not only in Latina theater but in world theater as well. From her loose experimental works of the early 1960s to the flourishing of her mature period as a dramatist, Fornes has staked her own unique claim on the forging of a new theatrical identity in Hispanic theater. Although she often cites Ibsen and Chekhov as her models, there is the undeniable stamp of Lorca's influence in her fluid dissection of time and space and of her characters' private and public personas, in the struggles her female heroines face, and in the hauntingly fatalistic endings she chooses for her plays.

Fornes draws less on Lorca's "theater of tomorrow" and more on the sense of repression, horror, blood, and beauty of his rural tragedies. In Mae's struggle to define herself in *Mud*, for instance, there is an echo of *The House of Bernarda Alba* and of Adela's desire to break free of her tyrannical world. In *Sarita*, Fornes' titular heroine struggles against her own sexual desire and the forces of machismo that ultimately, like in *Blood Wedding*, determine her fall. While this may be interpreted as reflective of a writer focusing on a specifically notorious aspect of Hispanic culture—its machismo, and women's continuing difficulty to break free of and through its pervasiveness—Fornes is canny enough as a playwright to draw on a tradition of writing that has come before her, and use that tradition to continue to explore women's roles in society and women's roles in theater.

> FELA: A woman like me
> loves a man,
> only one,
> and he must,
> run away.
> He must forsake her.
> He must forget her.
> He must betray her.
> And he must drink
> And die alone. [5]

Fornes also uses particularly "Lorcan" elements of image and song to propel a variety of her plays. In *Sarita*, Fela sings "A Woman Like Me" to ironically describe her social situation. And as young Marion hangs perilously from a rope in *Abingdon Square* reciting Dante to strengthen her spirit, the force of the image recalls Yerma's defiant "Que mi boca se quede muda" (May I never speak again).[6]

In fact, Fornes' *Abingdon Square* with its story of thwarted passion and self-discovery set in pre-World War I New York City is the most "Lorcan" of the plays in her oeuvre. With the impending changes of the women's movement as a backdrop, Fornes reconnects to a political sensibility that is powerful but never didactic or self-conscious. As Marion, the central character, searches for her own identity in other men, she slowly comes to terms with her own sexuality and individualism. Despite the confines of corsets and social codes, a society constricted by its own norms, the characters in *Abingdon Square* maintain a refreshing frankness of tone and spirit while speaking a language bold and delicate. There are sharp echoes of Lorca in Fornes' work, and in her now-trademark cutting of scenes into indelible snapshots—poems—of different moments in her characters' lives, she is able to dissect both literary time and theatrical time in a manner Lorca was only beginning to explore in *As Five Years Pass*.

Another writer based in New York who has been inspired by Lorca is the Bronx-born-and-bred Migdalia Cruz. She, along with José Rivera, is part of a generation of writers influenced by Fornes. Of Puerto Rican descent, Cruz explores with candor, feeling, and shocking intimacy the workings of characters at odds with life on the street, or characters who are caught in worlds that mirror or refract the world of fairy tales and historical novels. Moreover, she allows her characters to express their desires with an erotic fullness that allows for all taboos to be broken.

The gay and lesbian sensibility that is usually silenced in Latino culture comes to the fore in Cruz's work, as well as the work of an entire wave of Hispanic dramatists, who in looking for icons have found in Lorca the perfect gay "martyr" to fetishize and idolize. That Lorca's homosexual sensibility was more complex than simple coding will allow seems to be a small point to a gallery of writers who have taken up his name for a political and literary cause. Migdalia Cruz, however, does not fully belong to that gallery. She is more interested in what Lorca repressed in his writings, what was underneath the surface of his texts, and in making these subterranean forces take center stage in her work.

In her free adaptation of García Lorca's *The House of Bernarda Alba* entitled *Another Part of the House*, which premiered at Classic Stage Company in New York City in 1997, Cruz sets the action in Cuba in 1895 and makes the characters of Poncia and Maria Josefa the focal points for this re-telling of

Lorca's story. Poncia and Bernarda have an overtly homoerotic relationship, and there is an incestuous feeling in this Alba house as the sisters play their desires against each other. "For *Another Part of the House* [...] what I wanted to do was write all the unspoken stuff that Lorca didn't write—what I thought was underneath the play. I felt that I wrote around the subtext and its viscera as opposed to its outside world form," Cruz has stated.[7] Although this approach may strike purists as crude, Cruz's exploration of *The House of Bernarda Alba*'s subtext is a genuine reworking of Lorca's classic by a writer deeply influenced by his work. By making Poncia an Afro-Cuban slave, Cruz also heightens the class and racial divisions between servant and mistress, and thus makes their erotic union cross more than sexual boundaries.

> BERNARDA: Who taught you such a soothing touch? My fingers don't know how to move like that. You steal the pain right out of me.[8]

Migdalia Cruz offers her tribute to Lorca in the manner in which she builds on his characters' ignited passions and desires, and throughout her work, as she pushes her characters to confront each other in startling ways. Fusing her own sense of lyricism and beauty with Lorca's, she has created an emerging body of work that explores the savage and dark elements of the human psyche, creating a link to the brutal nature in much of the Iberian tragic canon.

Born in Puerto Rico but raised in New York, José Rivera has established his theatrical voice at the intersection of the old world and the new world, at the juncture of the Americas. Freely admitting to drawing inspiration from the magic-realist tradition as well as Lorca, Calderon de la Barca, and American pop culture, Rivera's work is at its core syncretic, romantic, and poetic.

Juxtaposing the suspended time of dreams and fantasy with the "real" time of average daily life, Rivera finds an elastic way to contain multiple realities on a single plane in his plays. Nowhere is this more evident than in his chamber piece *Cloud Tectonics*. Premiering at the Actors Theater of Louisville in 1995, *Cloud Tectonics* is a play about a mysterious pregnant young woman named Celestina del Sol and her encounter with a young man named Anibal de la Luna, who may or may not be her future son. Evocative of Lorca's *The Love of Don Perlimplín for Belisa in the Garden* and *As Five Years Pass*, Rivera creates a contemporary fable of romantic love that transcends time, even as it comments on it. Celestina is a character that functions as mother, lover, and sister in one. She is an echo of an echo of herself and of others' image of her.

CELESTINA: How do you know what time feels like, Anibal?...Is the organ for "time" the heart? Is it the spinal cord, that silver waterfall of nerves and memories... Does "time" have a sound? What bells, Anibal, what vibrating string played by that virtuoso accompanies the passage of time?... Or is it just the invisible freight train that runs over you every single day...pieces so small they can't hold soul to the earth anymore, and that's why you die? [9]

Rivera turns the question of time as it relates to the moments of conception, falling in love, even finding one's own language into a philosophical construct that holds his comic and tender play togther, much as Lorca does in the masterful and more ambitious work *As Five Years Pass*.

While Lorca was expansive and playful in his visual sensibility, and in his ability to combine ceremony with action, Rivera as younger, though established, Latino dramatist seeks to contain his worlds, even when they become nightmarish, as in his oft-produced play *Marisol*. A breakthrough of sorts for Rivera, *Marisol* is the play in which he allows himself as a writer to fully investigate the presentation of a world out of orbit. After early plays that toyed with notions of fluid time, ritual, and eroticism, *Marisol* uses the language of cyber-punk fiction to revitalize the idiom of Hispanic-American performance literature. Abandoned by her guardian angel, Marisol is caught in a Manhattan that is going up in flames, where a celestial Armageddon rages in the skies overhead. Recalling the more surreal elements of Lorca's miniatures *Buster Keaton Takes a Walk* and his film-script *A Trip to the Moon*, Rivera's play is contained by the totality of its commitment to the nightmare into which Marisol falls. A hellish picaresque, *Marisol* is kin to *Poet in New York* as it presents an illuminating contemporary meditation on the perilousness of human existence in a fractured, garbage-ridden world.

Fornes, Cruz, and Rivera represent different imaginative territories where the spirit of Lorca's work resides. Separated by age and temperament, these dramatists have pushed at the walls of mainstream theater in the United States, demanding, by their very nature, that Lorca's theatrical experiments of the 1920s and 1930s in Spain not be ignored. In so doing, they have encouraged a promising wave of younger Latino/a dramatists to seek their space both within and outside the margins set by mainstream culture. It can also be argued that generations of non-Latino U.S. dramatists influenced by Lorca have allowed for the development of a Latino theatrical sensibility. Tennessee Williams, Edward Albee, Sam Shepard, and Adrienne Kennedy have incorporated "Lorcan" concepts and references into their works, offering

Latino writers an opportunity to decode these references and seek out their origin, making of them what they will.

In a country where Lorca is virtually absent from the stage and relegated to the bookshelves and halls of universities' "ivory towers," transformation and transmutation have been the method by which Lorca's work has found a way to be seen and heard. Acts of ventriloquism and sleight-of-hand can be detected in the works of many a Hispanic and non-Latino playwright. It is credit to Lorca's genius that these acts of homage only deepen the search for his work to be truly represented. In the United States, Lorca waits to be discovered.

A VIEW FROM THE AMERICAS

If García Lorca is the great known / unknown presence in Hispanic-American performance literature, the rest of the Americas have been embracing his work and building on its foundation for a long time. García Lorca's trips to Cuba and Argentina in the 1930s and the performance history of his plays there and elsewhere in central and South America, spurred in part by actor Margarita Xirgu's theatrical ambassadorship of his work, have left an indelible mark on much of the theater that has emerged since the untimely death of the poet.

In Argentina, where the theatrical tradition has been linked to the erratic politics of the country as well as the strong influence of the European avant-garde, Griselda Gambaro has distinguished herself as one of the world's pre-eminent theatrical voices. Like her U.S. counterpart, Maria Irene Fornes, Gambaro uses an episodic "snapshot" structure to tell her stories of women abused by and triumphant against authority. Although Gambaro's work is deeply rooted in Argentina, she is markedly influenced by Lorca, Ionesco, Beckett, and Pinter. While her work hardly calls to mind Lorca's magic and delicacy, it does recall his poetry, heightened theatricality, unapologetic emotional power, and pre-feminist sensibility. As Lorca's work has been championed by various groups of political and intellectual thought, feminism has been linked to the "Lorcan" vocabulary since at least the early 1960s, before the word was codified and integrated into contemporary culture. The women in *The House of Bernarda Alba*, *Blood Wedding*, and *Yerma* have served as radical models for discussion and debate in feminist theatrical theory.

Playing at the intersection of Eros and Thanatos, Gambaro's theater not only places women at the center of the feminist question, but moves beyond that to examine, as Lorca did, how ingrained social roles have determined women's plight in relationship to the patriarchy. Whereas Lorca sent a defiant cry, Gambaro beats down the opposition, submitting it to her impassioned, idiosyncratic will. In a play like *Antigona Furiosa*, written in 1985–6, the first image is of Antigona hanged. As the play progresses in a timeless space, Antigona is both interrogator and interrogated. The members of the Chorus are two porteños sitting at a café and the play shifts between Antigona's moments of fury, usually in soliloquy, and the Chorus' mockingly ironic banter at her expense. It is a discomforting play, as is most of Gambaro's work, and it is one that fits squarely in a tradition of work by writers from the Americas that examines not only the question of the "woman in society," but also how one country's history can be inscribed into that of the world. Like Lorca's touchstone play *The House of Bernarda Alba*, *Antigona Furiosa*, though small in scale, is constructed around the paradigm of will vs. desire, action vs. inaction, violence vs. passivity. Gambaro wants her audience to bear witness to the cruelty that her characters suffer on stage, but she also wants to implicate her audience in the acts of cruelty. No one is exempt in Gambaro's theater. Not even the audience.

In one of her early plays from the 1960s *Las Paredes (The Walls)*, Gambaro focuses on a Young Man, not unlike Lorca's Young Man from *As Five Years Pass*, who is abducted upon returning home from a day in the country, and brought to an 1850s-style room, even though the time is the present. There are occasional screams offstage, and the Young Man is kept by an Usher and a Functionary in a room that is clearly a prison of some sort. As the play progresses, the room begins to vanish. An eerie, prescient play about the dilemma of the *desaparecidos* (disappeared) in Argentina, *Las Paredes*, which critic Diana Taylor has called exemplary of Gambaro's "theater of crisis" is a seductive, brutal play suffused with a feeling of death. *Las Paredes* uses space and time in as fictive a manner as Lorca and creates a world where past and present as fluid are as they are in memory.

While Gambaro explores violence, politics, and women's roles in society, poet / novelist / dramatist Ricardo Massa, who shares with Gambaro a long history in Argentine theater, works in a more surreal manner with similar subject matter. Less interested in creating roles for women, Massa explores the dream state as it relates to memory and the body politic.

In his performance text *La Trama de Sogas (Rope Plot)*, presented in Buenos Aires in 1988, Massa uses puppets, a complex multilayered sound score, and a dislocated scenario, where hats and ropes speak with a clown, a man, and his lover to present an anguished universe where the only solution to the erosion of a society's historical record vis à vis the public's personal memory is madness. Reminiscent of the more "impossible" theatrical notions posited by Lorca's *The Public*, as well as the commedia elements of *The Billy Club Puppets*, *La Trama de Sogas* is a tender, bitter, and hallucinatory piece of theater that is delicate and extreme, and very much a piece of "whole theater"—where the text is only an element of the *mise en scene*.

Chilean dramatist Ines Margarita Stranger belongs to a young generation of theater practitioners who also works within the notion of "whole theater." Often developing work collectively with a group of actors, Stranger is interested in the liminal space where the real and the symbolic collide, and in placing the female body at the center of the theatrical experience.

There is little doubt that Margarita Xirgu's arrival in Chile in 1938, and her stay in Santiago, where she founded her Academy of Dramatic Art, awoke in the Chilean public a love for the magic and poetry of García Lorca's theater. Xirgu's vital presence invigorated a theater that in the early 1930s was floundering, and which subsequent to her arrival, and those of other visiting artists like Louis Jouvet, flourished. Ines Margarita Stranger belongs to a new tradition of artists that are building on this vigorous foundation. A philosophical writer by nature, Stranger in her play *Cariño Malo (Bad Love)*, presented in Chile in 1990, creates a fluid theatrical environment where the private, interior space is presented as "real," and the public, exterior one as "surreal." Three women—Eva, Victoria, and Amapola—enact the various roles assigned to women in society as perceived by the male gaze. Ironic and poetic, *Cariño Malo* uses elements of song, cabaret, role playing, melodrama, and detailed sequences of visual action and image to explore the "bad love" of its title, the rage that women carry, and how passion and desire can trap but also liberate women from trying to be "what they're supposed to be."

Suffused with a homoerotic subtext, Stranger's work, which is firmly situated in the world of performance art in its sensibility, nevertheless bears the imprint of Lorca's influence in its use of signs and metaphors to tell its story rather than adhering to a more traditional nineteenth-century model, and in its focus on women's identity in society and the roles that they are asked to play in service to the patriarchy. Like the work of her contemporaries in the United States, Stranger benefits from Lorca's experiments to re-envision a hybrid theater for tomorrow.

If Lorca found in Cuba a measure of solace and joy, Cuban playwrights have paid considerable homage to him in their work over the years. Expatriated dramatist Eduardo Manet's extensive body of work both in Cuba and Paris have established him as one of the leading dramatists of the

Americas. His ritualized theatrical worlds that explore the idea of meta-theater or role playing within a role, his dark wit and Catholic sensibility link him inevitably to Lorca, as does the work of Jose Triana, another Cuban expatriate who found in Paris a place where he could put into perspective his lens of the Latin-American experience.

The varied and provocative work that has emerged in the Caribbean and Latin America owes much of its debt to the presence of García Lorca's work on their stages. The theater wrought in blood, fire, and sand in the 1920s and 1930s has become a part of the theatrical language in Central and South America, and its vocabulary continues to expand, while retaining its own elemental mystery.

THE PAST CONTAINS THE FUTURE

The slim book with the pencil-thin lettering that captured my imagination in the white-gray room of my high school days remains a constant source of inspiration and pleasure as I write today. The great poet that opened a window in my work, and offered me a glimpse of "deep song" sends his spirit shouting into the night. The words begin slowly, rising out of my throat: *alma, grito, duende.* And a hundred years of white roses and velvet thorns look down on me, withered petals in bloom on the head of a new-born poet. A new page begins. Another curtain rises. Where is Lorca this morning?

This essay was originally presented at the "100 Years of Lorca" Conference sponsored by Northern Stage in Newcastle, England 1998. A slightly modified version of this text can be found in the volume *Fire, Blood, and the Alphabet: 100 Years of Federico García Lorca*, Durham Modern Language Series, Durham University/UK, editors. M.P. Thompson and Sebastian Doggart, 1999.

Editions of plays referred to:

Cruz, Migdalia. *Another Part of the House*, unpublished playscript (1997).

Fornes, Maria Irene. *Maria Irene Fornes: Plays,* preface by Susan Sontag (New York: PAJ Publications, 1986).

_____. *Promenade and Other Plays* (New York: PAJ Publications, 1987).

Gambaro, Griselda. *Teatro 3* (Buenos Aires: Ediciones de la Flor, 1995).

Massa, Ricardo. *La trama de sogas* (Buenos Aires: Ediciones Teatro Istituto di Antropologia di Milano, 1988).

Rivera, Jose. *Cloud Tectonics* in *Marisol and Other Plays* (New York: TCG Publications, 1997).

Stranger, Ines Margarita. *Cariño Malo* in *Antologia bilingue de dramaturgia de mujeres latinoamericanas,* eds Graciela Ravetti and Sara Rojo (Belo Horizonte: Armazem de Ideias, 1996).

Svich, Caridad. *Alchemy of Desire / Dead-Man's Blues* in *Out of the Fringe*, eds Maria Teresa Marrero and Caridad Svich (New York: TCG Publications, 2000).

[1] Caridad Svich, *Alchemy of Desire / Dead-Man's Blues* in *Out of the Fringe: Contemporary Latina/o Theater and Performance*, Maria Teresa Marrero and Caridad Svich. Eds (New York: TCG Publications/Nick Hern Books, forthcoming February 2000).

[2] Ed Morales, "New World Order," *American Theater* (May/June 1998), 43.

[3] Lindy Zesch, "Viva Teatro!" *American Theater* (May/June 1998), 24.

[4] Maria Irene Fornes, *Maria Irene Fornes: Plays*, preface by Susan Sontag (New York: PAJ Publications, 1986), 104.

[5] Federico García Lorca, *Yerma, La casa de Bernarda Alba, Dona Rosita la soltera* (Madrid: Ediciones Novelas y Cuentos, 1974), 79.

[6] Daedalus Howell, "Play Right," *Sonoma County Independent* (30 October–5 November 1997), 3.

[7] Migdalia Cruz, *Another Part of the House*, unpublished playscript (1997)

[8] Jose Rivera, *Marisol and other Plays* (New York: TCG Publications, 1997), 21-22.

[9] Ibid.

NOTES ON *TRIP TO THE MOON*

Frederic Amat

One hundred years after the birth of Federico García Lorca, and after eventful mishaps and failed attempts to produce it, the time has come to screen publicly the poet's only film-script *Trip to the Moon*.

Written in New York, *Trip to the Moon* is a silent film that speaks for itself, a transformation of poetry into moving images that elude any narrative discourse. Lorca's script finds its meaning in the succession and contrast of scenes, and invites the viewer to reinvent a mosaic of allegorical images, a "theorem of the moon." In this unique medium-length filmmaking we find resonances with two other works that, together with *Trip to the Moon*, make up the trinity of Lorca's New York writings: the book of poems *Poet in New York* and the play *The Public*. As well as these three examples of literary creation, there is a constellation of drawings that illuminate the poet's American writings with elegant and unnerving expressivity. Joan Miró wrote of these drawings that "they seem to me the work of a great poet, that is the greatest praise I can give to any form of expression." In his screenplay for *Trip to the Moon*, the poet brings in another of his New York drawings: "Sequence 38: double exposure of bars passing over a drawing: Death of Saint Radegund."

Poems, theater, cinema, and drawings are woven together in a kaleidoscope of influences and echoes that help us unravel the poet's profound suggestion: his "truth of a man of blood," a visionary state of methodical creative delirium in which scenes and characters follow with apparent unease, but reveal a deep poetic logic. *Trip to the Moon* is not a tour of the unconscious; it is consciousness in anguished lucidity, it is the will to unmask a reality imposed as a monolith. The poet's attitude mirrors the spirit of surrealism, that last academy of revolution and rupture. It makes a brazen stance against reason, scandalizes bourgeois morality, and makes a bloody joke on stunted, stingy ways of thinking. Lorca shares the boldness of the avant-garde and its indignation at institutionalized hypocrisy, but in his New York work we are not in a dream of surrealist reason, but in a dialogue between dream and wakefulness, which takes place through an awareness of how living is like dying and how death is an extreme form of love. The fish biting its own tail; love and interruption implying death as episodes of accidental destiny. In Juliet's tomb, love does not conquer death; but "in the last resort, do Romeo and Juliet necessarily have to be a man and a woman for the scene to be produced in a cold and heartbreaking way?" Lorca makes this point through one of the characters in his play *The Public*. His proposal, subversive by the way, is the reconquest of love in its original state of innocence, far from any moral that might turn it into stagnant water, anchored instinct.

The poet's personal situation, woven with the threads of homosexual love, is a paradigm of both anguish and identity, "seed and ladder" of his poetic art. It cannot be reduced to a simple vindication of homosexual rights. His intention goes much further. It is an exaltation of love that is free, a love confronted by the values that repress instinct and that still graze and bleat through our valleys with masks of tolerance hiding faces of intransigence. *Trip to the Moon* is not just a trip inside the poet; it is also a universal journey. Through theater, poetry, and the cinema image, Lorca shows us a world of disguises, appearances, and masks, manifested in its true identity, naked and raw. The face in its final grimace: the skull.

There is no other God than god made man, he who turns his anguish into transforming sacrifice. The voice of the poet is plural; he takes the presence of that god that is mask-less, humanized, moved by amorous desire, a god who takes on bodily form, dies, and revives. "Centre stage, a bed, upright and facing downstage, like a primitive painting; on it, a red naked man, wearing a crown of blue thorns." This is how the fifth scene of *The Public* begins, with an image that recurs in *Trip to the Moon*: "The man with veins appears in the street and freezes as if crucified with his arms outstretched. He moves forward by jump cuts." We are in a cinema and a theater ruled by symbols as a store of knowledge. A cinema and a theater in which Lorca glimpses a new form of stage performance that at the same time drinks from the fountains of the Spanish *auto sacramental.*

The images of *Trip to the Moon* begin and end with a white bed, a kind of biographical allegory. At the start we see a "white bed against a grey wall. A dance of the numbers 13 and 22 takes place on the bedclothes. From two figures, they begin to multiply like tiny ants." In the final scenes "a bed appears and hands covering a dead man." The numerology is not random:

"Love, love, love," neigh the three horses in *The Public*. "Love of the one with the two and love of the three which is suffocated by being one between two." 13 and 22, two ages of adolescence and youth that are represented in two of the film's scenes. As in many of García Lorca's drawings, we contemplate characters with split identities. The *Trip to the Moon* is not a spatial voyage; it is a journey through the poetic mirror of time and light that is the moon of cold silver and hidden shadow of water.

For years a sombre curse has hung over attempts to gain complete knowledge and an exact location of Lorca's American manuscripts. Specialists and scholars have written pages and pages of doubts, approximations, and brilliant ideas on the subject. In the case of *Poet in New York*, the mystery begins with the first publication of the work in 1940, through José Bergamín in Mexico and the Norton edition in New York. Who guards the manuscript that Lorca gave Bergamín in 1936 and today is thought to be in Mexico? Did Bergamín alter the order of poems? Many other mysteries surround his play *The Public*, unedited until publication in the 1970s, through the lucid studies of Rafael Martínez Nadal, the friend to whom Lorca entrusted the manuscript before embarking on his last trip to Granada, where he would be assassinated a few weeks later. This piece of theater, impossible though not unperformable, finally premiered on December 12, 1986, in the Piccolo Theater in Milan under Lluís Pasqual's direction, with costumes and set created by Fabià Puigserver, with my collaboration.

Three years later, in 1989, there appeared in Oklahoma, forgotten at the back of a drawer, the original script for *Trip to the Moon*. Until then, only inexact translations had been known. Found were seventy-two scenes written by Lorca on small diary pages for the painter Emilio Amero, whom he got to know during his stay in New York. Spurred on by the experiences of the avant-garde, Amero invited the poet to write a film-script. Lorca was certainly aware of the poetic, dynamic, and psychoanalytical possibilities of the camera and must also have felt stimulated by seeing many prodigious works created in the then-innovative medium of cinema. The script for *Trip to the Moon* shows awareness of the ideas of Eisenstein about montage as a collision of confrontational sequences, of the visions of Buster Keaton, Friedrich Murnau, Vsevolod Pudovkin, Erich von Stroheim, and Abel Gance; and of the visual rhythms of 1920s avant-garde filmmakers like René Clair, Man Ray, Marcel Duchamp, and Fernand Léger. In that decade, painting and film found a fertile communion through the intention of revealing time through light and composition. Cinema made it possible, through movement, to visualize the convulsive acceleration of a new technological and urban society.

Machines appear on the screen as abstract automatons, confronted with the human, rural world, to which Lorca had always felt attached.

During Lorca's stay in New York, his friends Buñuel and Dalí, presented in Paris the film *Un chien andalou*, an extraordinary and innovative combination of poetic and filmic images. The poet probably never saw the film, but we know that he was angry at what he considered to be a personal slight, through a remark that Ian Gibson quotes in his invaluable biography of Lorca: "Buñuel has made a weensy little shit of a film called *An Andalusian Dog*, and I am the dog."

Beyond veneration for the film as a relic, disentangling the glittering enigmas of *Trip to the Moon* by re-creating its images has been a fascinating task for me. An undertaking to distill its essence, to silhouettte its poetic suggestions, to apply different filmic processes to let the script itself reveal Lorca's own conception, secretive and inexplicable, but in no way unintelligible. Making the poet's idea visible allows us to see pictorial, filmic processes of virtual reality and of image editing. His unusual approach makes it appropriate to use, without anachronism, both the virtual technology of the late twentieth century and more traditional forms. It is a representation of representations in which the drawn is juxtaposed with the filmed. His magnetic images must be allowed to flow to an exact rhythm, to reveal the world of desire and its frustration, on a voyage that takes us from the microcosm to the reflection of the stars: the freedom of man to "build his desire through coral vein or heavenly nude; tomorrow, loves will be rocks and time a sleeping breeze through the branches."

CONTRIBUTORS

FREDERIC AMAT is a painter, scenic designer, and filmmaker based in Barcelona. He has worked extensively with noted Catalan stage director (and García Lorca specialist) Lluís Pasqual, among others. *Viaje a la luna / Trip to the Moon* (1998) is his first film.

LISSETTE CAMACHO is a Ph.D. candidate at Rutgers University.

JIM CARMODY teaches dramatic literature and theater history at the University of California—San Diego, where he heads the new PhD program in Theater and Drama. He is the author of *Rereading Moliere: Mise en Scene from Antoine to Vitez*, and he is currently working on a volume of contemporary French theater. He is co-editor of the international theater magazine *TheaterForum*.

MARIA DELGADO is Lecturer in the School of English and Drama at Queen Mary and Westfield College, the University of London. She is the translator of *Valle-Inclan Plays: One* (London: Methuen, 1993 and 1997); editor of the recent edition of *Contemporary Theater Review* entitled "Spanish Theater 1920–95: Strategies in Protest and Imagination;" co-editor of *In Contact with the Gods?: Directors Talk Theater* (Manchester University Press, 1996) and *Conducting a Life: Reflections on Theater of Maria Irene Fornes* (Smith & Kraus, 1999).

ERIK EHN is married to scenic artist Pat Chanteloube, the charge at the Berkeley Rep. Ehn's plays include *Heavenly Shades of Night Are Falling, Wolf at the Door, The Moon of Scarlet Plums, The Sainte Plays, Erotic Curtsies,* and *Chokecherry.* He is a graduate of New Dramatists.

PAUL JULIAN SMITH is the Professor of Spanish and Head of the Department of Spanish and Portuguese at Cambridge University. He has published ten books on Spanish and Spanish-American literature, theater, and cinema including *The Theater of García Lorca: Text, Performance, Psychoanalysis* (Cambridge University Press, 1998), *Desire Unlimited: The Cinema of Pedro Almodovar* (second edition Verso, 2000); and *The Moderns: Time, Space, and Subjectivity in Contemporary Spanish Culture* (Oxford University Press, 2000).

COLIN TEEVAN was born in Dublin. His original stage plays include *The Big Sea, Tear Up the Black Sail, Buffalo Bill Has Gone to Alaska,* and most recently *Svejk.* He has translated for the stage from several European languages, most recently *Marathon* and *Cuckoos* from Italian, which have been produced at the Gate Theater, London. He is published by Oberon Books and Nick Hern Books. He is co-founder and former artistic director of Galloglass Theater Company, Ireland. In 1997, he was appointed Writer-in-Residence at Queen's University, Belfast, where he is now Head of Drama.

SARAH WRIGHT completed her doctorate at Clare Hall, Cambridge and currently works as Lecturer in the Department of Hispanic Studies at the University of Hull, England. She is the author of *The Trickster-Function in the Theater of García Lorca* (Tamesis, 2000).

INDEX

CARIDAD SVICH is an affiliated playwright at the Mark Taper Forum Theatre in Los Angeles, where she previously held an NEA/TCG Residency. Credits include her play with songs *Alchemy of Desire / Dead-Man's Blues,* which premiered at Cincinnati Playhouse in the Park as winner of the Rosenthal New Play Prize, and *Any Place But Here,* which was seen at Theater for the New City in New York under the direction of Maria Irene Fornes. Other plays include *Fugitive Pieces* (a play with songs) at Kitchen Dog Theater in Dallas, Texas, and *The Archaeology of Dreams* that was workshopped at Portland Stage Company's Little Festival of the Unexpected. She has been a guest artist at the Traverse Theatre in Edinburgh, the Royal Court Theatre, and has taught playwriting at the Yale School of Drama, Paines Plough Theatre in London, and the US-Cuba Writers' Conference in Havana. Her play *Gleaning/Rebusca* can be found in the anthology *Shattering the Myth* (Arte Publico Press), and her music-theater piece *Brazo Gitano* in the magazine *Ollantay.* She is co-editor of *Conducting a Life: Reflections on the Theater of Maria Irene Fornes* (Smith & Kraus), and *Out of the Fringe: Contemporary Latina/o Theatre and Performance* (TCG Books). She is a member of New Dramatists.